DEVELOPING THE FRUIT OF PATIENCE LONGSUFFERING

30 DAY DEVOTIONAL

SUZANNE PHILLIPPA MARCELLUS

All scripture is taken from the King James Version of the Bible.

Editor:	Phillip Washington Fender
Cover Design:	Teodore Thomas
Photo on Back:	Jeaneane Swaby of ThruJensEyes
ISBN:	978-0-9976864-2-5

PREFACE

This devotional will help refine your character, as you allow the Fruit of Patience Longsuffering to be cultivated in your life.

In Chapter 8 of *Developing the Fruit of the Spirit, A Journey Through the Heart of Christ*, the foundation is laid for the development of patience.

"This next fruit we will discuss is Makrothymia. In Galatians 5:22, this Greek word is translated as longsuffering or patience, depending on your preferred translation of the Bible. In other scripture passages it is translated as endurance, constancy, steadfastness, perseverance, forbearance, and slowness in avenging wrongs. The sufferings and challenges that produce patience are the sour times in our lives. I sought out a fruit that by its very name, created a clear picture of the journey the development of this fruit takes on. I chose the delicious Soursop. Like longsuffering, the outside of the Soursop's bitter skin is covered in prickles that soften once ripened. Although longsuffering can be a bitter process, it should not make you a bitter person. As you cut pass the bitter skin, inside this tropical fruit you'll enjoy a creamy, white, sweet somewhat tangy pulp, filled with multiple medicinal properties. It is believed by many, although not yet proven medically, to aid in the cure of cancer." (Marcellus, Developing the Fruit of the Spirit, A Journey Through the Heart of Christ, p.93)

The Hebrew transliteration of the name of our Heavenly Father, YHWH, translated as Yahweh (normally translated in English as Jehovah or "the Lord") and the Hebrew name for Jesus our Messiah, Yahshua, is used in this devotional.

How Do I Use this Devotional?

I am thankful that our Heavenly Father led you to this devotional. I pray you experience the growth you are seeking in Him. To assist you in evaluating your progress, I have included a Personal Evaluation Form for your use on Days 1, 15 and 30.

Each day will begin with the same prayer, which is based on the Our Father's Prayer taught to us by Yahshua in Matthew 6:9-13. It will be followed by two pages of truths from the Word of Yahweh with opportunities to search and examine your heart.

You will be challenged to see the beauty in yourself as you examine the ugly places in your soul, that Yahweh wants to heal and transform. To make your process more fruitful, be honest with yourself and with Yahshua.

In the first four chapters of _Developing the Fruit of the Spirit, A Journey Through the Heart of Christ,_ I go into great detail on:

1. Evaluating the condition of the soil of your soul, based on Matthew 13:18-23. The condition of your soil determines the speed and sustainability of your growth.
2. The necessity of Repentance. Without it, we become spiritually dead and can bear no good fruit.
3. The importance of Forgiveness. We must first forgive others and ourselves, before we can receive forgiveness from our Heavenly Father.
4. Examining your present fruit. Yahweh pays attention to both the good and bad fruit we bear. Daily examine yourself against His Word.

It is vital to keep these things in mind as you continue your journey. Allow Holy Spirit to speak to you as you open your heart to Him.

PERSONAL EVALUATION

How often do you...	Never	Sometimes	Always
Obey Yahweh?			
Reflect on how patient Yahweh is with you?			
Give up on/Lose hope in the promises of Yahweh?			
Walk in Your Identity?			
Struggle with being impatient?			
Struggle with idolatry?			
Suffer for wrong doing?			
Suffer for doing what is right?			
Resist temptation?			
Mistreat others when having a difficult day?			
Have a joyous attitude during a difficult day?			
Feel overwhelmed by difficult times?			
Rest in the Lord as you wait on Him?			
Grow tired of doing what's right?			
Depend on Holy Spirit?			
Wear the Armour of Yahweh?			

What does patience look like to you?

_____

_____

_____

_____

_____

Day One

Our Lord waits patiently on us.

Heavenly Father, You are holy, I glorify You in the beauty of Your Holiness. Thank you for loving, protecting, caring and providing for my family and me. When times are good, I will praise you! When times are difficult, I will praise you! I will honor and exalt You in every circumstance.

Let your kingdom come and will be done in my life, as it is in Heaven. Cause your purpose to be fulfilled in me. I choose to seek you first and invite Precious Holy Spirit to develop His fruit in my life.

Continue to provide for my family, friends, neighbors, and myself all that we need today. May there be more than enough to share with others.

Search my heart, and show me what hidden sin is in my life. As I confess each one to you, purify me in Your presence and create in me a clean heart and renew a right spirit within me.

I forgive my enemies and friends who have hurt, angered, offended or betrayed me and ask that you would have mercy on them and bless them.

Please forgive me of all my evil thoughts, words and actions. I recognize that my sin hurts, angers, offends and betrays You.

Teach me your ways, that I might not sin against You. Inscribe Your word on my heart and mind, that all of my ways, would be pleasing to you.

Do not lead me into temptation, but deliver me from all evil.

To you, Oh Mighty Yahweh, belongs the kingdom, the power and the glory, in Yahshua's name.

...Behold, the husbandman waiteth for the precious fruit of the earth, and hath long patience for it, until he receive the early and latter rain. James 5:7

Have you ever considered that on many occasions Yahweh has had to wait patiently on you? When He gives us instructions, often we delay in stepping out in faith and obeying Him. Maybe it's a vision He has given you to accomplish, but it is so large, that you run from the very purpose for which you were created. Perhaps, it's what we consider to be the little things, He's waiting on, like being kind, loving and patient with others. Our Heavenly Father, the husbandman, awaits His fruit to be developed in our lives. He sees the *fruit as precious*, while patiently waiting on the harvest that the early and latter rain bring.

Several weeks before writing this journal, my patience felt stretched past its limit. I was so frustrated, that I broke down in a loud cry to the Lord. My children were convinced that they had finally pushed me over the edge of sanity. Then it hit me like a lightning bolt, *"It's time to write again, and you must begin with Patience Longsuffering."*

The fire revealed the maturity of the fruit of patience in my life and pointed me in the direction of Yahshua's leading, which previously I was too distracted to notice.

Has Yahweh been waiting on you; is there something He has asked you to do or stop doing that you have not obeyed?

_____

_____

Would you be frustrated, annoyed and given up on yourself by now, if you had to wait on yourself as long as Yahweh has waited on you?

_____

Come, and let us return unto the LORD: for he hath torn, and he will heal us; he hath smitten, and he will bind us up. ² After two days will he revive us: in the third day he will raise us up, and we shall live in his sight. ³ Then shall we know, if we follow on to know the LORD: his going forth is prepared as the morning; and he shall come unto us as the rain, as the latter and former rain unto the earth.
Hosea 6:1-3

Hosea 6 begins with a call of repentance, inviting us to return to the Lord and be healed, fixed, revived, raised up and living in His sight. He is The Rain that causes us to grow and bear fruit that are pleasing to Him. Yahweh is waiting for the manifestation of His character and Spirit to be seen in us. He asks us to be just as patient when we wait on Him, as He is, when He patiently waits on us.

Be patient therefore, brethren, unto the coming of the Lord...Be ye also patient; stablish your hearts: for the coming of the Lord draweth nigh.
James 5:7-8

Some people complain saying, *"I've heard my entire life that Yahshua is coming soon, but He hasn't come yet!"* Somehow, His delay causes quite a large number in the body of Christ to lose their sense of urgency and conviction to live holy and non-compromising lifestyles.

Are you a part of that number? If you are, repent. Now, steady your heart as you wait on His return. Don't be distracted and delayed by the issues of life. Be still in the confident hope that what you go through is not in vain. Confess, in Yahshua's name, that you will produce a harvest for the Lord and that you will receive a harvest from Him.

For we are saved by hope: but hope that is seen is not hope: for what a man seeth, why doth he yet hope for? ²⁵ But if we hope for that we see not, then do we with patience wait for it. Romans 8:24-25

Day Two

The Lord's Longsuffering is Salvation.

Heavenly Father, You are holy, I glorify You in the
beauty of Your Holiness. Thank you for loving,
protecting, caring and providing for my family and me.
When times are good, I will praise you! When times are
difficult, I will praise you! I will honor and exalt You in
every circumstance.

Let your kingdom come and will be done in my life, as it
is in Heaven. Cause your purpose to be fulfilled in me. I
choose to seek you first and invite Precious Holy Spirit
to develop His fruit in my life.

Continue to provide for my family, friends, neighbors,
and myself all that we need today. May there be more
than enough to share with others.

Search my heart, and show me what hidden sin is in my
life. As I confess each one to you, purify me in Your
presence and create in me a clean heart and renew a
right spirit within me.

I forgive my enemies and friends who have hurt,
angered, offended or betrayed me and ask that you
would have mercy on them and bless them.

Please forgive me of all my evil thoughts, words and
actions. I recognize that my sin hurts, angers, offends
and betrays You.

Teach me your ways, that I might not sin against You.
Inscribe Your word on my heart and mind, that all of my
ways, would be pleasing to you.

Do not lead me into temptation, but deliver me from all
evil.

To you, Oh Mighty Yahweh, belongs the kingdom, the
power and the glory, in Yahshua's name.

But, beloved, be not ignorant of this one thing, that one day is with the Lord as a thousand years, and a thousand years as one day. 2 Peter 3:8

At any point of your life, has it felt like you have been waiting on Yahweh seemingly forever? I have often felt this way. Since one thousand years are equivalent to one of His days, His timeline and ours are obviously very different. By the age of 41 you have only lived *one hour* of your life on Yahweh's timeline. Isn't that amazing?

"And, behold, I come quickly; and my reward is with me, to give every man according as his work shall be." Revelation 22:12

2,000 years ago our Lord declared His return was soon. Yet, by His time clock, it has only been 2 days.

Yahweh is in eternity, knowing our beginning and end. He sees our life before we've lived it. Surely when He says something good is going to happen for us, it is because He has already:

Decreed, Established, and Fulfilled It.

Isn't it awesome that He knows more about our future than we can ever imagine? Truly His ways are not our ways and His thoughts are not our thoughts.

Do you believe that Yahweh's timing is perfect?

The Lord is not slack concerning his promise, as some men count slackness; but is longsuffering to us-ward, not willing that any should perish, but that all should come to repentance. 2 Peter 3:9

Have you ever considered that the miracle you are waiting on, may be the point of contact with heaven others need, to come to repentance, salvation, deliverance, or to increase their faith? His timing is always perfect with a bigger picture at hand, than what we initially see.

Is there a request you have presented to the Lord that involves someone being blessed through your blessing?

_____

_____

And account that <u>the longsuffering of our Lord is salvation</u>; even as our beloved brother Paul also according to the wisdom given unto him hath written unto you; 2 Peter 3:15

Wisdom shouts, *"The Lord's Longsuffering is Salvation!"*

➢ If Yahweh had not been patient with all of creation, He would have destroyed us all in the flood. Instead, He saved Noah, his family and the animals.
➢ If He had not been longsuffering with the Hebrews in the wilderness after He delivered them from Egypt, an entire nation would have been delivered only to be destroyed.
➢ If He had not sent Yahshua and allowed Him to suffer and die for each one of us, we would have been eternally condemned.

Thank Yahweh, that He is a patient longsuffering Savior!

He models patience longsuffering for us, so we may follow His example.

Since the Lord is longsuffering towards you and all people, will you chose to be more patient with yourself and others?

_____

_____

Day Three

Creation Waits Patiently on Us.

Heavenly Father, You are holy, I glorify You in the beauty of Your Holiness. Thank you for loving, protecting, caring and providing for my family and me. When times are good, I will praise you! When times are difficult, I will praise you! I will honor and exalt You in every circumstance.

Let your kingdom come and will be done in my life, as it is in Heaven. Cause your purpose to be fulfilled in me. I choose to seek you first and invite Precious Holy Spirit to develop His fruit in my life.

Continue to provide for my family, friends, neighbors, and myself all that we need today. May there be more than enough to share with others.

Search my heart, and show me what hidden sin is in my life. As I confess each one to you, purify me in Your presence and create in me a clean heart and renew a right spirit within me.

I forgive my enemies and friends who have hurt, angered, offended or betrayed me and ask that you would have mercy on them and bless them.

Please forgive me of all my evil thoughts, words and actions. I recognize that my sin hurts, angers, offends and betrays You.

Teach me your ways, that I might not sin against You. Inscribe Your word on my heart and mind, that all of my ways, would be pleasing to you.

Do not lead me into temptation, but deliver me from all evil.

To you, Oh Mighty Yahweh, belongs the kingdom, the power and the glory, in Yahshua's name.

It is not only us who are called to wait patiently on Yahweh, or Him, who waits patiently on us; there is another group who is waiting. All of creation is waiting on us to realize, believe and walk in who we are in Yahshua. When Adam and Eve fell in the Garden of Eden, the consequence of death impacted all of creation, not just humanity.

> **And unto Adam he said, because thou hast hearkened unto the voice of thy wife, and hast eaten of the tree, of which I commanded thee, saying, thou shalt not eat of it: cursed is the ground for thy sake; in sorrow shalt thou eat of it all the days of thy life; Genesis 3:17**

The ground from which we were formed was cursed to make our lives laborious. The authority entrusted to us by Yahweh to care for all that He made was compromised.

If the ground could speak, what do you think it would have said to Adam and Eve?

_____

> **_For the earnest expectation of the creature waiteth for the manifestation of the sons of God._ 20 For the creature was made subject to vanity, not willingly, but by reason of him who hath subjected the same in hope, 21 Because the creature itself also shall be delivered from the bondage of corruption into the glorious liberty of the children of God. 22 _For we know that the whole creation groaneth and travaileth in pain together until now._ 23 And not only they, but ourselves also, which have the firstfruits of the Spirit, even we ourselves groan within ourselves, waiting for the adoption, to wit, the redemption of our body. Romans 8:19-23**

How does it feel to know that creation is waiting on you to know who you are in Christ?

_____

Numbers 22 records the story of the donkey who spoke. Yahweh opened her mouth so she could question her master, Balaam. He had hit her three times because she did not walk in the direction he had commanded. Unlike Balaam, she could SEE the Angel of the Lord, who was appointed to kill him, because of his sin.

This donkey knew, that had she walked to where the angel stood, her master would have died. Her revelation protected him, she saved his life. Balaam did not see the angel, until the Lord opened his eyes.

Imagine, creation has a revelation that currently many of us cannot SEE or understand. Romans 8 says it groans and travails in pain, waiting on the sons of Yahweh to be manifested.

Creation realizes that through our deliverance and transformation comes its' deliverance and transformation.

Does this impact the way you view creation?

_____

_____

Does this change the way you view yourself?

_____

_____

If creation can be patient, what is your excuse?

_____

_____

Heavenly Father, please open my eyes to see who I am in Christ. Give me the faith to believe that I am valuable and important in Your Kingdom. Manifest Yourself through me, in Yahshua's name.

Day Four

Impatience leads you to disobedience and idolatry.

Heavenly Father, You are holy, I glorify You in the
beauty of Your Holiness. Thank you for loving,
protecting, caring and providing for my family and me.
When times are good, I will praise you! When times are
difficult, I will praise you! I will honor and exalt You in
every circumstance.

Let your kingdom come and will be done in my life, as it
is in Heaven. Cause your purpose to be fulfilled in me. I
choose to seek you first and invite Precious Holy Spirit
to develop His fruit in my life.

Continue to provide for my family, friends, neighbors,
and myself all that we need today. May there be more
than enough to share with others.

Search my heart, and show me what hidden sin is in my
life. As I confess each one to you, purify me in Your
presence and create in me a clean heart and renew a
right spirit within me.

I forgive my enemies and friends who have hurt,
angered, offended or betrayed me and ask that you
would have mercy on them and bless them.

Please forgive me of all my evil thoughts, words and
actions. I recognize that my sin hurts, angers, offends
and betrays You.

Teach me your ways, that I might not sin against You.
Inscribe Your word on my heart and mind, that all of my
ways, would be pleasing to you.

Do not lead me into temptation, but deliver me from all
evil.

To you, Oh Mighty Yahweh, belongs the kingdom, the
power and the glory, in Yahshua's name.

In 1 Samuel 13:8-14, we observe Saul getting impatient as he waited seven days for Samuel to arrive and present an offering to the Lord, on behalf of himself and the people. Out of his FEAR of the Philistines, Saul decided to present the offering himself. His impatience resulted in an act that was in direct disobedience to the command the Lord had given him.

Since Yahweh has not given us a spirit of fear, we must not make decisions from a panicked state of mind. Learn to wait on Yahweh, even when you think He is running late.

Listen to Samuel's response in 1 Samuel 13:13-14, when he arrived on the scene,

"And Samuel said to Saul, thou hast done foolishly: thou hast not kept the commandment of the LORD thy God, which he commanded thee: for now would the LORD have established thy kingdom upon Israel for ever. 14 But now thy kingdom shall not continue: the LORD hath sought him a man after his own heart, and the LORD hath commanded him to be captain over his people, because thou hast not kept that which the LORD commanded thee."

Although Saul was permitted to rule Israel for forty-two years, it was during his second year of leadership that he forfeited the throne for his generations to come.

Have you considered the impact your impatience could have on your children?

_____

Did you know that there are consequences for moving ahead of Yahweh's timing?

_____

Exodus 32 shows how the impatience of the Israelites led them to idolatry. While Moses was on the mountain for

17

forty days and forty nights, the people saw the manifestation of the presence of Yahweh like a devouring fire on the top of the mountain (Exodus 24). Though they witnessed our Lord's presence and power, Moses' return was just taking *too long.*

Impatience led to:

> ➤ The *"brilliant idea"* of manufacturing their own god, a golden calf.
> ➤ The belief that their man-made god would be able to do the same things Yahweh had done for them.

And the LORD said unto Moses, Go, get thee down; for thy people, which thou broughtest out of the land of Egypt, have corrupted themselves: 8 They have turned aside quickly out of the way which I commanded them: they have made them a molten calf, and have worshipped it, and have sacrificed thereunto, and said, these be thy gods, O Israel, which have brought thee up out of the land of Egypt. Exodus 32:7-8

What manmade god (idol) have you created and attributed Yahweh's glory to, in your times of impatience?

_____

_____

"Our idols are anyone or anything we put before Yahweh. It's important to continue to trust God even when our hearts grow discouraged in times of waiting." (Marcellus, Developing the Fruit of the Spirit, A Journey Through the Heart of Christ, p.110)

Heavenly Father, I repent of my impatience that has led me to disobedience and idolatry. Please forgive me for moving ahead of you in my times of fear and anxiety. I renounce fear, anxiety and every idol that I have created in place of You. I choose You, in Yahshua's name.

Day Five

Why Are You Suffering?

Heavenly Father, You are holy, I glorify You in the beauty of Your Holiness. Thank you for loving, protecting, caring and providing for my family and me. When times are good, I will praise you! When times are difficult, I will praise you! I will honor and exalt You in every circumstance.

Let your kingdom come and will be done in my life, as it is in Heaven. Cause your purpose to be fulfilled in me. I choose to seek you first and invite Precious Holy Spirit to develop His fruit in my life.

Continue to provide for my family, friends, neighbors, and myself all that we need today. May there be more than enough to share with others.

Search my heart, and show me what hidden sin is in my life. As I confess each one to you, purify me in Your presence and create in me a clean heart and renew a right spirit within me.

I forgive my enemies and friends who have hurt, angered, offended or betrayed me and ask that you would have mercy on them and bless them.

Please forgive me of all my evil thoughts, words and actions. I recognize that my sin hurts, angers, offends and betrays You.

Teach me your ways, that I might not sin against You. Inscribe Your word on my heart and mind, that all of my ways, would be pleasing to you.

Do not lead me into temptation, but deliver me from all evil.

To you, Oh Mighty Yahweh, belongs the kingdom, the power and the glory, in Yahshua's name.

During difficult times in our lives, we tend to ask, *"Why is this happening to me? Why am I suffering?"* Scripture teaches us that as followers of Christ, we will not elude suffering. Suffering comes with the territory of dying to our sinful nature. There are two main categories of suffering. We suffer as a consequence of sin in our lives or because of righteous living.

But let none of you suffer as a murderer, or as a thief, or as an evildoer, or as a busybody in other men's matters. 1 Peter 4:15

Today is a good day to give yourself an honest inventory. It's important to examine every area of your life through the light of Yahweh's truth.

Are some of the struggles and hardships you're enduring a result of decisions you have made?

We have all acted out of anger, lust, and deceit (the list could go on) at some point in our lives. *When we recognize we are suffering because of sin, we can repent, forgive ourselves and others and ask Yahweh for forgiveness.* As a result, we retrieve the key to the door of our lives from the enemy and place it back into the hands of our loving Savior, Yahshua.

For what glory is it, if, when ye be buffeted for your faults, ye shall take it patiently? but if, when ye do well, and suffer for it, ye take it patiently, this is acceptable with God. 1 Peter 2:20

What has suffering for righteousness looked like in your life?

Have you felt ashamed during times of suffering for Christ?

_____

_____

Yet if any man suffer as a Christian, let him not be ashamed; but let him glorify God on this behalf.
1 Peter 4:16

It is difficult when people mock, misunderstand, wrongly judge, speak evil of and hate you. Rejection does not feel good for anyone, yet the Apostle Peter encourages us to glorify Yahweh in these moments.

What does it mean to glorify God on behalf of your suffering?

_____

_____

Each time you praise, adore, worship, exalt, and give honor and reverence to Yahweh, you glorify Him. Peter is telling us to praise the Lord amid our suffering. *These are not the moments to meltdown or have temper tantrums but our opportunities to cry out in praise to our Heavenly Father.*

Suggestion: Find at least one song that provokes you to worship whether things are going great or challenges are arising in your life. During difficult times, don't listen to music that will feed your disappointments, pain and sorrow. Listen to and sing your pre-chosen song from the depths of your soul until there is a shift in your emotions. *Encourage yourself in the Lord, so that you will not sin against Him during your assigned seasons of suffering.*

Wherefore let them that suffer according to the will of God commit the keeping of their souls to him in well doing, as unto a faithful Creator. 1 Peter 4:19

Day Six

Don't be surprised if you are called to suffer.

Heavenly Father, You are holy, I glorify You in the beauty of Your Holiness. Thank you for loving, protecting, caring and providing for my family and me. When times are good, I will praise you! When times are difficult, I will praise you! I will honor and exalt You in every circumstance.

Let your kingdom come and will be done in my life, as it is in Heaven. Cause your purpose to be fulfilled in me. I choose to seek you first and invite Precious Holy Spirit to develop His fruit in my life.

Continue to provide for my family, friends, neighbors, and myself all that we need today. May there be more than enough to share with others.

Search my heart, and show me what hidden sin is in my life. As I confess each one to you, purify me in Your presence and create in me a clean heart and renew a right spirit within me.

I forgive my enemies and friends who have hurt, angered, offended or betrayed me and ask that you would have mercy on them and bless them.

Please forgive me of all my evil thoughts, words and actions. I recognize that my sin hurts, angers, offends and betrays You.

Teach me your ways, that I might not sin against You. Inscribe Your word on my heart and mind, that all of my ways, would be pleasing to you.

Do not lead me into temptation, but deliver me from all evil.

To you, Oh Mighty Yahweh, belongs the kingdom, the power and the glory, in Yahshua's name.

***Beloved, think it not strange concerning the fiery
trial which is to try you, as though some strange
thing happened unto you: 1 Peter 4:12***

Although we neither want nor care for trials, we should
not be shocked, when they come knocking at our door.
Peter explains that their purpose is to TRY US! Trials
make us feel disrespected and powerless because we do
not get to choose their expiration date. They cease when
Yahweh says, "CEASE".

Are you surprised, each time you face a difficult season
in your life?

_____

If yes, why? Do you think every believer and follower of
Christ should be excused from hardships?

_____

_____

What expectations do you have of your relationship with
Yahshua? Should each day be trouble free? If so, who
taught you that, was it Him?

_____

_____

It is important to identify any flaws in the foundation that
was laid in your faith in Christ. It can determine whether
you withstand the storms of life with Him as your anchor
or if you decide that this Christian life isn't for you.
Yahshua guaranteed that we would have trouble while we
live in this world and called us to rejoice in these times.

***But rejoice, inasmuch as ye are partakers of
Christ's sufferings; that, when his glory shall be
revealed, ye may be glad also with exceeding joy.
1 Peter 4:13***

23

Your suffering in Him reveals HIS GLORY!

If ye be reproached for the name of Christ, happy
are ye; for the spirit of glory and of God resteth
upon you: on their part he is evil spoken of, but on
your part he is glorified. 1 Peter 4:14

Our times of suffering for Christ should excite us because it invites the Spirit of Glory and of Yahweh to rest on us, as He did on Yahshua. It is humbling to know that as our inner man is transformed in the fire, there is an outward manifestation of His Glory.

Your suffering is a magnet for His presence!

What does it mean to you, to have Yahweh's Spirit and Glory rest on you, when you suffer for Christ?

_____

_____

_____

There may be times when people will perceive you the same way Job's friends perceived him. Wondering what you've done to deserve such hardships as they wrongly accuse and judge you. Do not be discouraged. In Matthew 27:43 as Yahshua hung on the cross, the crowds taunted Him, saying,

"He trusted in God; let him deliver him now, if he
will have him: for he said, I am the Son of God."

When our Heavenly Father does not rescue us according to the timeline and perspective of ourselves and others, the enemy wants us to doubt our identity as loved, accepted and forgiven children of Yahweh.

Yahweh raised Yahshua from the dead and His Spirit lives in us. Regardless of your circumstance *you are already VICTORIOUS!*

24

Day Seven

Don't be afraid to suffer for what is right.

Heavenly Father, You are holy, I glorify You in the beauty of Your Holiness. Thank you for loving, protecting, caring and providing for my family and me. When times are good, I will praise you! When times are difficult, I will praise you! I will honor and exalt You in every circumstance.

Let your kingdom come and will be done in my life, as it is in Heaven. Cause your purpose to be fulfilled in me. I choose to seek you first and invite Precious Holy Spirit to develop His fruit in my life.

Continue to provide for my family, friends, neighbors, and myself all that we need today. May there be more than enough to share with others.

Search my heart, and show me what hidden sin is in my life. As I confess each one to you, purify me in Your presence and create in me a clean heart and renew a right spirit within me.

I forgive my enemies and friends who have hurt, angered, offended or betrayed me and ask that you would have mercy on them and bless them.

Please forgive me of all my evil thoughts, words and actions. I recognize that my sin hurts, angers, offends and betrays You.

Teach me your ways, that I might not sin against You. Inscribe Your word on my heart and mind, that all of my ways, would be pleasing to you.

Do not lead me into temptation, but deliver me from all evil.

To you, Oh Mighty Yahweh, belongs the kingdom, the power and the glory, in Yahshua's name.

Have you come to terms with the fact that suffering for the sake of righteousness is the will of our Heavenly Father?

For it is better, <u>if the will of God be so</u>, that ye suffer for well doing, than for evil doing. ¹⁸ For Christ also hath once suffered for sins, the just for the unjust, that he might bring us to God, being put to death in the flesh, but quickened by the Spirit: 1 Peter 3:17-18

Yahweh willed for Yahshua to suffer and die, it was through His suffering that we were reconciled to Him. When we are called to suffer, our carnality is crucified and maturation takes place.

Our suffering matures us into His likeness.

Who his own self bare our sins in his own body on the tree, that we, being dead to sins, should live unto righteousness: by whose stripes ye were healed. ²⁵ For ye were as sheep going astray; but are now returned unto the Shepherd and Bishop of your souls. 1 Peter 2:24-25

Yahshua is the Shepherd and Bishop of our souls! Psalm 23 is a beautiful description of how our Shepherd leads us, even in the valley moments of our lives.

The LORD is my shepherd; I shall not want. ² He maketh me to lie down in green pastures: he leadeth me beside the still waters. ³ He restoreth my soul: he leadeth me in the paths of righteousness for his name's sake. ⁴ <u>Yea, though I walk through the valley of the shadow of death, I will fear no evil: for thou art with me; thy rod and thy staff they comfort me.</u> ⁵ Thou preparest a table before me in the presence of mine enemies: thou anointest my head with oil; my cup runneth over.

⁶ Surely goodness and mercy shall follow me all the days of my life: and I will dwell in the house of the LORD for ever.

Verse 4 highlights the suffering of our journey in Christ, while the others solidify our faith that He will continue to provide, bring peace, guide, restore, anoint and cause our enemies to see His blessings, goodness and mercy shine in our lives. Since He is with us, we do not have to be afraid as we walk through the valley of the shadow of death, His rod and His staff continually comfort us.

Does the thought of suffering bring you fear, anxiety and sadness?

_____

_____

***And who is he that will harm you, if ye be followers of that which is good? ¹⁴ But and if ye suffer for righteousness' sake, happy are ye: and be not afraid of their terror, neither be troubled;
1 Peter 3:13-14***

Do you believe it is possible to have joy, peace and courage during difficult times in your life?

_____

_____

Yahweh's love, peace and joy surpass all our human understanding. When you suffer, allow Holy Spirit to make your heart still without a trace of anxiety. His love casts out all fear and gives us the courage we need to press on as His joy becomes our strength. Always remember Yahshua in the Garden of Gethsemane.

Heavenly Father, make me unafraid to suffer, fill me with Your courage, peace, love and joy in Yahshua's name.

Day Eight

Christ left us an example of suffering.

Heavenly Father, You are holy, I glorify You in the beauty of Your Holiness. Thank you for loving, protecting, caring and providing for my family and me. When times are good, I will praise you! When times are difficult, I will praise you! I will honor and exalt You in every circumstance.

Let your kingdom come and will be done in my life, as it is in Heaven. Cause your purpose to be fulfilled in me. I choose to seek you first and invite Precious Holy Spirit to develop His fruit in my life.

Continue to provide for my family, friends, neighbors, and myself all that we need today. May there be more than enough to share with others.

Search my heart, and show me what hidden sin is in my life. As I confess each one to you, purify me in Your presence and create in me a clean heart and renew a right spirit within me.

I forgive my enemies and friends who have hurt, angered, offended or betrayed me and ask that you would have mercy on them and bless them.

Please forgive me of all my evil thoughts, words and actions. I recognize that my sin hurts, angers, offends and betrays You.

Teach me your ways, that I might not sin against You. Inscribe Your word on my heart and mind, that all of my ways, would be pleasing to you.

Do not lead me into temptation, but deliver me from all evil.

To you, Oh Mighty Yahweh, belongs the kingdom, the power and the glory, in Yahshua's name.

Yahshua relates with every moment of our lives because He walked in the same flesh body that we do, His was no different. He left us the steps to follow in our times of suffering.

> *For even hereunto were ye called: because Christ also suffered for us, leaving us an example, that ye should follow his steps: 22 Who did no sin, neither was guile found in his mouth: 23 Who, when he was reviled, reviled not again; when he suffered, he threatened not; but committed himself to him that judgeth righteously: 1 Peter 2:21-23*

Let's review His steps:
1. He did not sin through action or speech, nor did He lie.
2. When He was spoken to angrily and abusively, He did not reciprocate to his revilers with like language.
3. He did not try to get revenge on those by whose hands He suffered. Instead He committed himself to Yahweh, knowing that He is the Righteous Judge and vengeance belongs to Him alone.

When you suffer:

Do you end up falling into sin? If yes, how so?

_____

_____

Do you reciprocate abuse shown to you? If yes, how so?

_____

_____

Do you get revenge or plot ways to do so? If yes, how so?

_____

_____

You might have answered these questions, while thinking to yourself, "of course I've done all of the above, I'm not Yahshua!" It's a challenge, isn't it? None of us are Him, yet when we invite Him to make us a new creation, we give Him permission to transform us.

Longsuffering is a process that we are called to partake in, if it wasn't, Yahshua wouldn't have wasted His time modelling suffering for us. Yahweh could have chosen any other way to reconcile us to Himself, but He chose death. Or did we; that day in the garden when Adam and Eve ate the fruit from the forbidden tree of Knowledge of Good and Evil?

> *Forasmuch then as the children are partakers of flesh and blood, he also himself likewise took part of the same; that through death he might destroy him that had the power of death, that is, the devil; 15 and deliver them who through fear of death were all their lifetime subject to bondage.*
> *Hebrews 2:14-15*

Because of Christ's death we are free from a lifetime of bondage. We are no longer subject to the devil nor the fear of death.

> *And if children, then heirs; heirs of God, and joint-heirs with Christ; if so be that we suffer with him, that we may be also glorified together. 18 For I reckon that the sufferings of this present time are not worthy to be compared with the glory which shall be revealed in us. Romans 8:17-18*

As we suffer with Him we are glorified with Him. *Suffering produces glory!* In times of suffering remind yourself that those moments are incomparable to the glory which will be revealed in you.

Christ the HOPE OF GLORY!

Day Nine

Temptation is a type of suffering.

Heavenly Father, You are holy, I glorify You in the
beauty of Your Holiness. Thank you for loving,
protecting, caring and providing for my family and me.
When times are good, I will praise you! When times are
difficult, I will praise you! I will honor and exalt You in
every circumstance.

Let your kingdom come and will be done in my life, as it
is in Heaven. Cause your purpose to be fulfilled in me. I
choose to seek you first and invite Precious Holy Spirit
to develop His fruit in my life.

Continue to provide for my family, friends, neighbors,
and myself all that we need today. May there be more
than enough to share with others.

Search my heart, and show me what hidden sin is in my
life. As I confess each one to you, purify me in Your
presence and create in me a clean heart and renew a
right spirit within me.

I forgive my enemies and friends who have hurt,
angered, offended or betrayed me and ask that you
would have mercy on them and bless them.

Please forgive me of all my evil thoughts, words and
actions. I recognize that my sin hurts, angers, offends
and betrays You.

Teach me your ways, that I might not sin against You.
Inscribe Your word on my heart and mind, that all of my
ways, would be pleasing to you.

Do not lead me into temptation, but deliver me from all
evil.

To you, Oh Mighty Yahweh, belongs the kingdom, the
power and the glory, in Yahshua's name.

Did you know that temptation is a type of suffering?

"Wherefore in all things it behoved him to be made like unto his brethren, that he might be a merciful and faithful high priest in things pertaining to God, to make reconciliation for the sins of the people. 18 For in that <u>he himself hath suffered being tempted, he is able to succour them that are tempted.</u>" Hebrews 2:17-18

Since Yahshua suffered being tempted, not only does He relate with us, but He helps us during times of temptation.

What are your current temptations?

_____

Would you like His help to overcome them?

_____

Repeated sin in a believer's life produces a mindset that says, *"Yahweh is ok with my sin, He'll forgive me since He knows this is my area of weakness. I'm covered by His grace."* Yes, He forgives and He is gracious, but He does not approve of us being content in our weaknesses. In Christ we have been designed to not only endure but to overcome temptation.

Blessed is the man that endureth temptation: for when he is tried, he shall receive the crown of life, which the Lord hath promised to them that love him. James 1:12

Temptations test our faith. As Yahshua was led into the wilderness by Holy Spirit, He was tempted by the tempter, Satan, for 40 days (Matthew 4 and Luke 4). If our Savior's faith had to be tested through temptation of hunger, suicide, power, worship of another and more, we need to be ready to resist the devil, just as He did.

For we have not an high priest which cannot be touched with the feeling of our infirmities; but was in all points tempted like as we are, yet without sin. Hebrews 4:15

Is it possible to be tempted as Christ was, yet not sin?

_____

Submit yourselves therefore to God. Resist the devil, and he will flee from you. James 4:7

What areas of your life do you still need to submit to God?

_____

How will you resist the devil? (Yahshua resisted him with the WORD of YAHWEH)

_____

_____

Let no man say when he is tempted, I am tempted of God: for God cannot be tempted with evil, neither tempteth he any man: <u>*14 But every man is tempted, when he is drawn away of his own lust, and enticed. 15 Then when lust hath conceived, it bringeth forth sin: and sin, when it is finished, bringeth forth death.*</u> *16 Do not err, my beloved brethren." James 1:13-16*

Talk to the Lord about your temptations. Repent and ask for forgiveness for the times when you were drawn away from Him by your own lust, which gave birth to sin. Lust is a seed that you don't want planted, watered or fertilized in the SOIL of your SOUL. You must be prepared when the tempter comes to derail you or when your own soul desires things outside of the parameters, Yahweh has set for your protection. Study Yahweh's Word and hide it in your heart so you can use it as your WEAPON.

Day Ten

Arm Yourself with the Mind of Christ.

Heavenly Father, You are holy, I glorify You in the beauty of Your Holiness. Thank you for loving, protecting, caring and providing for my family and me. When times are good, I will praise you! When times are difficult, I will praise you! I will honor and exalt You in every circumstance.

Let your kingdom come and will be done in my life, as it is in Heaven. Cause your purpose to be fulfilled in me. I choose to seek you first and invite Precious Holy Spirit to develop His fruit in my life.

Continue to provide for my family, friends, neighbors, and myself all that we need today. May there be more than enough to share with others.

Search my heart, and show me what hidden sin is in my life. As I confess each one to you, purify me in Your presence and create in me a clean heart and renew a right spirit within me.

I forgive my enemies and friends who have hurt, angered, offended or betrayed me and ask that you would have mercy on them and bless them.

Please forgive me of all my evil thoughts, words and actions. I recognize that my sin hurts, angers, offends and betrays You.

Teach me your ways, that I might not sin against You. Inscribe Your word on my heart and mind, that all of my ways, would be pleasing to you.

Do not lead me into temptation, but deliver me from all evil.

To you, Oh Mighty Yahweh, belongs the kingdom, the power and the glory, in Yahshua's name.

"Forasmuch then as Christ hath suffered for us in the flesh, arm yourselves likewise with the same mind: for he that hath suffered in the flesh hath ceased from sin; 2 That he no longer should live the rest of his time in the flesh to the lusts of men, but to the will of God." 1 Peter 4:1-2

It is crucial that we have the mind of Christ during our times of suffering. *Begin to view your hard times as gifts used by our Heavenly Father to remove your sin nature.* We are dying so that Christ can live through us. We are being fortified to do the will of our Heavenly Father.

Let this mind be in you, which was also in Christ Jesus: Philippians 2:5

When I compare the mind of Christ to mine, I examine myself:
> ➢ How do His thoughts differ from mine?
> ➢ How does His worldview differ from mine?
> ➢ How does His view of our Heavenly Father differ from mine?
> ➢ How does His understanding of longsuffering differ from mine?

How does your mind differ from the mind of Christ?

_____

_____

When going through challenging times, what thoughts plague you?

_____

_____

And be not conformed to this world: but be ye transformed by the renewing of your mind, that ye may prove what is that good, and acceptable, and perfect, will of God. - Romans 12:2

Do you want to be conformed to this world more than you want your mind to be renewed?

_____

As your mind is renewed, Yahweh's will for your life will become more discernable. Don't invite insecurities, self-doubt or hardships to move in with you. If they show up, uninvited, don't entertain them by feeding them thoughts that will cause them to grow. Meditate on the Word of Yahweh to overcome their lies with His truth. As He leads you, follow. You won't have to break down doors to get your promises, in His time He will open the doors and walk you through them.

For ye have need of patience, that, after ye have done the will of God, ye might receive the promise.
Hebrews 10:36

What is the will of God for your life?

_____

_____

As you study Scripture, you will know the will of God for every believer in Yahshua. Through time spent in prayer, you will have a clearer picture of your specific purpose, the reason He created you.

It is helpful to pay attention to the areas He has always drawn you to. You have the solution to someone's problem, you may be their encourager, provider, teacher, mentor, inventor, intercessor, technician, doctor, pastor, parent...

Who are you?

_____

Your moments of developing patience will reveal your identity in Christ.

Day Eleven

Do not mistreat others in your times of suffering.

Heavenly Father, You are holy, I glorify You in the
beauty of Your Holiness. Thank you for loving,
protecting, caring and providing for my family and me.
When times are good, I will praise you! When times are
difficult, I will praise you! I will honor and exalt You in
every circumstance.

Let your kingdom come and will be done in my life, as it
is in Heaven. Cause your purpose to be fulfilled in me. I
choose to seek you first and invite Precious Holy Spirit
to develop His fruit in my life.

Continue to provide for my family, friends, neighbors,
and myself all that we need today. May there be more
than enough to share with others.

Search my heart, and show me what hidden sin is in my
life. As I confess each one to you, purify me in Your
presence and create in me a clean heart and renew a
right spirit within me.

I forgive my enemies and friends who have hurt,
angered, offended or betrayed me and ask that you
would have mercy on them and bless them.

Please forgive me of all my evil thoughts, words and
actions. I recognize that my sin hurts, angers, offends
and betrays You.

Teach me your ways, that I might not sin against You.
Inscribe Your word on my heart and mind, that all of my
ways, would be pleasing to you.

Do not lead me into temptation, but deliver me from all
evil.

To you, Oh Mighty Yahweh, belongs the kingdom, the
power and the glory, in Yahshua's name.

When the ugliness in our souls is brought to the surface by the fire of our suffering, we have two choices.

1. Allow Holy Spirit to scoop it off.
2. Simmer in frustration and let the bubbles of muck spill over and burn those around us.

On a day when patience is being worked on in my soul, you're guaranteed to see a less pleasant side of me. The process exposes the ugliness in my heart, as my secret negative thoughts, seep off my tongue. Frustration levels rise as my brain signals its' imminent explosion.

Can you relate?

It's as if the Lord knows the exact button to push to remind us that our sin nature is in daily need of sanctification.

Having therefore these promises, dearly beloved, let us cleanse ourselves from all filthiness of the flesh and spirit, perfecting holiness in the fear of God.
2 Corinthians 7:1

What are the buttons that when pushed, cause you to think, "I'm about to lose my Christianity"?

_____

Examine each of these buttons and ask yourself:

1. Why do these things/people/places provoke me to this level?

_____

_____

Somehow it's easier to identify what others need to change in their lives than it is to confront how we poorly handle hardships, conflicts and disappointments.

2. What personal changes can I make so as not to give these "buttons" power over my internal/external reactions?

_____

_____

3. What personal changes can I make so as not to give these "buttons" power over my faith in Yahshua?

_____

_____

James 5:9 warns us,

Grudge not one against another, brethren, lest ye be condemned: behold, the judge standeth before the door.

Yahweh is constantly watching, listening and observing the genuineness of our faith. Treat and speak of others kindly and forgive quickly.

It is vital that we learn to walk through life without a grudge on our shoulder. Grudges carry an odor, like that of a rotten egg. They can alter your physical appearance making misery one of your facial features. No fruit of Yahweh's Spirit looks like MISERY.

Will you allow Yahweh to scoop off the ugliness in your soul?

_____

Heavenly Father, please forgive me for the times I've spewed filth over the lives of others. Take away the desire to complain, embrace misery and dwell on negativity. Come and scoop away the filth in my life, in Yahshua's Holy name.

Day Twelve

Suffer with joy and patience.

Heavenly Father, You are holy, I glorify You in the beauty of Your Holiness. Thank you for loving, protecting, caring and providing for my family and me. When times are good, I will praise you! When times are difficult, I will praise you! I will honor and exalt You in every circumstance.

Let your kingdom come and will be done in my life, as it is in Heaven. Cause your purpose to be fulfilled in me. I choose to seek you first and invite Precious Holy Spirit to develop His fruit in my life.

Continue to provide for my family, friends, neighbors, and myself all that we need today. May there be more than enough to share with others.

Search my heart, and show me what hidden sin is in my life. As I confess each one to you, purify me in Your presence and create in me a clean heart and renew a right spirit within me.

I forgive my enemies and friends who have hurt, angered, offended or betrayed me and ask that you would have mercy on them and bless them.

Please forgive me of all my evil thoughts, words and actions. I recognize that my sin hurts, angers, offends and betrays You.

Teach me your ways, that I might not sin against You. Inscribe Your word on my heart and mind, that all of my ways, would be pleasing to you.

Do not lead me into temptation, but deliver me from all evil.

To you, Oh Mighty Yahweh, belongs the kingdom, the power and the glory, in Yahshua's name.

As seen in scripture, Yahweh's prophets set a pure example of suffering with joy. This resulted in them experiencing His tender mercy. We must learn how to suffer with joy and patience.

Take, my brethren, the prophets, who have spoken in the name of the Lord, for an example of suffering affliction, and of patience. 11 Behold, we count them happy which endure. Ye have heard of the patience of Job, and have seen the end of the Lord; that the Lord is very pitiful, and of tender mercy.
James 5:10-11

Is there a prophet or person in Scripture, who inspires you by the way he/she suffered with patience? Who is it?

_____

What do you think their secret was to maintain joy as they endured?

_____

_____

_____

At the beginning of Psalm 103, King David, commanded his soul to bless the Lord. He continued,

"But the mercy of the LORD is from everlasting to everlasting upon them that fear him, and his righteousness unto children's children; 18 to such as keep his covenant, and to those that remember his commandments to do them." Psalm 103:17-18

I believe the secret is...
  ➤ *Having FAITH IN THE LORD.*
  ➤ *Having the FEAR OF THE LORD.*
  ➤ *Having a heart committed to OBEY THE LORD.*

Yahweh invites us to Fear Him and no one else. It is here, where you:

1. Reverence and honor Him in the beauty of His holiness.
2. Make up your mind to obey Him, no matter the cost. Why? Because the proof of our love for Him is our obedience to Him.
3. Can endure suffering, believing that Yahweh will fulfill all of His promises. *It's either we will believe He is who He says He is or wrestle with the fact that we may still be an unbeliever.*

Often our discouragement and sadness are fruits of hopelessness. There is an internal or external voice speaking to us, as Job's wife, saying "curse God and die". The voice sees no hope for our future. We have a choice to believe the voice of the enemy or trust the voice of Yahweh. Job trusted Yahweh in such an immovable way that he said,

Though he slay me, yet will I trust in him: but I will maintain mine own ways before him. Job 13:15

Whose voice(s) are you listening to and believing?

_____

_____

Blessed is that man that maketh the LORD his trust, and respecteth not the proud, nor such as turn aside to lies. Psalm 40:4

Heavenly Father, forgive me for believing the lies spoken over my life. I choose to listen, believe and obey only Your voice. I break the bondage of those lies through the BLOOD OF YAHSHUA. Place in me a Holy Fear of You. Let every part of my life honor You. Thank You for blessing me as You did Job, in Yahshua's name.

"So the LORD blessed the latter end of Job more than his beginning:" Job 42:12

Day Thirteen

Be sober and vigilant in your times of suffering.

Heavenly Father, You are holy, I glorify You in the beauty of Your Holiness. Thank you for loving, protecting, caring and providing for my family and me. When times are good, I will praise you! When times are difficult, I will praise you! I will honor and exalt You in every circumstance.

Let your kingdom come and will be done in my life, as it is in Heaven. Cause your purpose to be fulfilled in me. I choose to seek you first and invite Precious Holy Spirit to develop His fruit in my life.

Continue to provide for my family, friends, neighbors, and myself all that we need today. May there be more than enough to share with others.

Search my heart, and show me what hidden sin is in my life. As I confess each one to you, purify me in Your presence and create in me a clean heart and renew a right spirit within me.

I forgive my enemies and friends who have hurt, angered, offended or betrayed me and ask that you would have mercy on them and bless them.

Please forgive me of all my evil thoughts, words and actions. I recognize that my sin hurts, angers, offends and betrays You.

Teach me your ways, that I might not sin against You. Inscribe Your word on my heart and mind, that all of my ways, would be pleasing to you.

Do not lead me into temptation, but deliver me from all evil.

To you, Oh Mighty Yahweh, belongs the kingdom, the power and the glory, in Yahshua's name.

Our enemy, the devil, is always attempting to distract us from keeping our focus on Yahshua. He looks for opportunities to gain legal ground in our lives, where we unknowingly give him the keys to different areas of our domain (personal holiness, family, marriage, children, ministry, property...). It is for this reason that we must always be alert, standing against him, filled with faith.

Do you believe that unrepentant sin gives the enemy permission to wreck some things in your life?

_____

_____

_____

Be sober, be vigilant; because your adversary the devil, as a roaring lion, walketh about, seeking whom he may devour: 1 Peter 5:8

We cannot become so lackadaisical that we let our spiritual guards down. The enemy is not one we can see with our natural eyes, so to discern his tactics, we must walk in the Spirit of Yahweh. There are times that our sufferings drain us of our strength to persevere, if not careful, confusion starts to set in.

Can you recall a time where you felt intoxicated by the pain and fear you experienced in your time of afflictions?

_____

_____

_____

When Apostle Peter, tells us to be sober, he is calling forth clarity and stability of mind. Consider this, a drunk person is not only a danger to themselves but a danger to all in their path.

How can you move from a place of having no control over your emotions to having a sober and vigilant mind?

_____

_____

_____

Whom resist stedfast in the faith, knowing that the same afflictions are accomplished in your brethren that are in the world. 1 Peter 5:9

As the enemy meets us along the path of our suffering, we are called to have unwavering, immovable faith in Yahshua. Sometimes we think we are the only ones suffering, and from this perspective we can take on the "woe is me" mentality. **You are not the only one.** Every believer is walking down the path of longsuffering our Heavenly Father has chosen for us, whether we are transparent about it or not. *It makes sense that we are processed together, since we are all a part of one body, YAHSHUA'S BODY. The body must be made complete together.*

But the God of all grace, who hath called us unto his eternal glory by Christ Jesus, after that ye have suffered a while, <u>make you perfect, stablish, strengthen, settle you.</u> 1 Peter 5:10

Praise Yahweh, our suffering will not last forever! The beauty in all the ashes of our suffering is, *they are working out something excellent in our lives.* Did you know that wood ashes are important for plant health, when gardening? They contain trace minerals that are needed for the plant and the soil. Our suffering contains the necessary minerals we need to produce the Fruit of the Spirit.

It Perfects us,
Establishes us,
Strengthens us and
Settles us!

45

Day Fourteen

Let Patience Have Its Perfect Work.

Heavenly Father, You are holy, I glorify You in the beauty of Your Holiness. Thank you for loving, protecting, caring and providing for my family and me. When times are good, I will praise you! When times are difficult, I will praise you! I will honor and exalt You in every circumstance.

Let your kingdom come and will be done in my life, as it is in Heaven. Cause your purpose to be fulfilled in me. I choose to seek you first and invite Precious Holy Spirit to develop His fruit in my life.

Continue to provide for my family, friends, neighbors, and myself all that we need today. May there be more than enough to share with others.

Search my heart, and show me what hidden sin is in my life. As I confess each one to you, purify me in Your presence and create in me a clean heart and renew a right spirit within me.

I forgive my enemies and friends who have hurt, angered, offended or betrayed me and ask that you would have mercy on them and bless them.

Please forgive me of all my evil thoughts, words and actions. I recognize that my sin hurts, angers, offends and betrays You.

Teach me your ways, that I might not sin against You. Inscribe Your word on my heart and mind, that all of my ways, would be pleasing to you.

Do not lead me into temptation, but deliver me from all evil.

To you, Oh Mighty Yahweh, belongs the kingdom, the power and the glory, in Yahshua's name.

Our perception of the times in our lives that are the most challenging, will determine how fast we walk through the battlefield. And yes, I said walk through, not fly over. We expect our Heavenly Father to deliver us from evil, just as He has promised, but what if the thing, person or situation we are classifying as evil, is actually placed in our lives by Yahweh, to TEST our FAITH?

Knowing this, that the <u>trying of your faith</u> worketh patience. James 1:3

The fruit of Faith and the fruit of Patience go hand in hand. The Lord uses the trials in our lives, to show us how mature and stable our Faith is, in Him.

That the <u>trial of your faith</u>, being much more precious than of gold that perisheth, though it be tried with fire, might be found unto praise and honour and glory at the appearing of Jesus Christ: ⁹ Receiving the end of your faith, even the salvation of your souls. 1 Peter 1:7, 9

As you answer the following two questions, be honest with yourself. Use this time to ask the Lord to forgive you of all of your doubts and fears and replace them with His love and peace. Just whisper, "*Increase my faith Yahweh, and please help my unbelief, in Yahshua's name*".

Have any of your trials:

    1. Provoked you to trust more in Yahshua?

_____

    2. Caused you to question Yahweh's existence?

_____

    3. Caused you to question His love for you?

_____

4. Caused you to question the promises He has spoken over your life in His Word?

_____

The trial of your faith is more precious than gold. When gold is melted, its' impurities are separated by extreme heat, which rise to the surface. *How much more will the fire that is used to refine our faith, separate the impurities in us?* The fire of our trials will feel like extreme heat at times; *let it do its job.* When we meet Yahshua face to face, our faith will bring Him praise, honor and glory, before our words can.

The fires of our suffering perfect us. The book of Hebrews teaches that Yahshua, the Captain of our Salvation, was MADE PERFECT through His sufferings.

> ***For it became him, for whom are all things, and by whom are all things, in bringing many sons unto glory, to make the captain of their salvation perfect through sufferings.* 11 *For both he that sanctifieth and they who are sanctified are all of one: for which cause he is not ashamed to call them brethren, Hebrews 2:10-11***

Why is the Lord so concerned about producing the fruit of Patience Longsuffering that He allows us to suffer?

_____

_____

> ***But let patience have her perfect work, that ye may be perfect and entire, wanting nothing. James 1:4***

James says we will lack nothing once patience completes its' work in us.

Will you let patience have its perfect work in you?

_____

Day Fifteen

Rest in the Lord, free from fear, anger and jealousy.

Heavenly Father, You are holy, I glorify You in the
beauty of Your Holiness. Thank you for loving,
protecting, caring and providing for my family and me.
When times are good, I will praise you! When times are
difficult, I will praise you! I will honor and exalt You in
every circumstance.

Let your kingdom come and will be done in my life, as it
is in Heaven. Cause your purpose to be fulfilled in me. I
choose to seek you first and invite Precious Holy Spirit
to develop His fruit in my life.

Continue to provide for my family, friends, neighbors,
and myself all that we need today. May there be more
than enough to share with others.

Search my heart, and show me what hidden sin is in my
life. As I confess each one to you, purify me in Your
presence and create in me a clean heart and renew a
right spirit within me.

I forgive my enemies and friends who have hurt,
angered, offended or betrayed me and ask that you
would have mercy on them and bless them.

Please forgive me of all my evil thoughts, words and
actions. I recognize that my sin hurts, angers, offends
and betrays You.

Teach me your ways, that I might not sin against You.
Inscribe Your word on my heart and mind, that all of my
ways, would be pleasing to you.

Do not lead me into temptation, but deliver me from all
evil.

To you, Oh Mighty Yahweh, belongs the kingdom, the
power and the glory, in Yahshua's name.

Our impatience shines as we wait on Yahweh to answer our prayers, fulfill promises or rescue us from unwanted circumstances. In these moments, we may become envious of the success of others and disappointed at the delay of the manifestation of our provision.

> *Rest in the LORD, and wait patiently for him: fret not thyself because of him who prospereth in his way, because of the man who bringeth wicked devices to pass. Psalm 37:7*

Have you become jealous or angry while observing someone's life who prospers through unrighteous gain, without having to suffer? Asking, "*Why do they get it so easy? Where's your judgment Lord? Why does my road have to be so hard? I thought doing what was right would secure me an easy life.*"

Can you relate to any of the thoughts above?

_____

Have you ever been angry with the Lord, because someone seems to have an easier lot in life than you?

_____

Release any anger you have with the Lord and with those getting ahead in life through ungodly ways. Repent for the times you've compromised or considered compromising your faith for money, fame or comfort.

> *Cease from anger, and forsake wrath: fret not thyself in any wise to do evil. ⁹ For evildoers shall be cut off: but <u>those that wait upon the LORD, they shall inherit the earth</u>. Psalm 37:8-9*

Yahweh is a Righteous Judge and He rewards His children with an earthly inheritance. *Walk in the Way, Will and Timing of the Lord.*

Or despisest thou the riches of his goodness and forbearance and longsuffering; not knowing that the goodness of God leadeth thee to repentance?
Romans 2:4

Our Heavenly Father desires for all to come to the saving knowledge of Christ. We are called to genuinely pray for those, who we perceive to be our enemies. Unfortunately, not everyone accepts Yahshua's invitation. The Lord is not blind to the motives of an evil heart and in His time, the wicked will be dealt with accordingly.

Wait on the LORD, and keep his way, and he shall exalt thee to inherit the land: when the wicked are cut off, thou shalt see it. Psalm 37:34

We must practice resting in the Lord. The Hebrew word used for *rest* in this verse is *damam*, meaning to be still and silent. Ask Holy Spirit to make you comfortable being quiet in Yahweh's presence as you expectantly wait on Him to answer you.

What does resting in the Lord mean and look like to you?

_____

Come unto me, all ye that labour and are heavy laden, and <u>I will give you rest</u>. 29 Take my yoke upon you, and learn of me; for I am meek and lowly in heart: and ye shall find rest unto your souls. 30 For my yoke is easy, and my burden is light. Matthew 11:28-30

Yahshua wants to teach us how to rest from our work and burdens, by clothing our hearts in His meekness and humility. *Truly, He is our Rest.* We have an open invitation to cast our cares on Him, daily.

What changes do you need to make in your daily routine to help you rest in Yahshua?

_____

PERSONAL EVALUATION

How often do you...	Never	Sometimes	Always
Obey Yahweh?			
Reflect on how patient Yahweh is with you?			
Give up on/Lose hope in the promises of Yahweh?			
Walk in Your Identity?			
Struggle with being impatient?			
Struggle with idolatry?			
Suffer for wrong doing?			
Suffer for doing what is right?			
Resist temptation?			
Mistreat others when having a difficult day?			
Have a joyous attitude during a difficult day?			
Feel overwhelmed by difficult times?			
Rest in the Lord as you wait on Him?			
Grow tired of doing what's right?			
Depend on Holy Spirit?			
Wear the Armour of Yahweh?			

How has Holy Spirit changed or challenged you in the above areas?

_____

_____

_____

_____

Day Sixteen

Continue to do what is righteous as you wait.

Heavenly Father, You are holy, I glorify You in the beauty of Your Holiness. Thank you for loving, protecting, caring and providing for my family and me. When times are good, I will praise you! When times are difficult, I will praise you! I will honor and exalt You in every circumstance.

Let your kingdom come and will be done in my life, as it is in Heaven. Cause your purpose to be fulfilled in me. I choose to seek you first and invite Precious Holy Spirit to develop His fruit in my life.

Continue to provide for my family, friends, neighbors, and myself all that we need today. May there be more than enough to share with others.

Search my heart, and show me what hidden sin is in my life. As I confess each one to you, purify me in Your presence and create in me a clean heart and renew a right spirit within me.

I forgive my enemies and friends who have hurt, angered, offended or betrayed me and ask that you would have mercy on them and bless them.

Please forgive me of all my evil thoughts, words and actions. I recognize that my sin hurts, angers, offends and betrays You.

Teach me your ways, that I might not sin against You. Inscribe Your word on my heart and mind, that all of my ways, would be pleasing to you.

Do not lead me into temptation, but deliver me from all evil.

To you, Oh Mighty Yahweh, belongs the kingdom, the power and the glory, in Yahshua's name.

***But after thy hardness and impenitent heart
treasurest up unto thyself wrath against the day of
wrath and revelation of the righteous judgment of
God; Romans 2:5***

Have you been getting away with a hidden sinful lifestyle? If your answer is yes and it appears that no one has knowledge of it, I need you to know that Yahweh is very much aware. We will all have to account for every word spoken and deed done, when we stand before His throne on judgment day. Let today be the end of your double life. I assure you, He will forgive, cleanse, deliver, heal and transform you.

***Who will render to every man according to his
deeds: Romans 2:6***

Will you be rewarded for your perseverance? Never giving up on the promises of Yahweh, thereby continuously doing what is right in His sight as you press towards eternal life.

***To them who by <u>patient continuance</u> in well doing
seek for glory and honour and immortality,
eternal life: Romans 2:7***

Why do you think, patience is necessary to help us to continue to do what is right?

_____

_____

Have there been times in your life, when everything in you wanted to go against a righteous path? How difficult was it to not give in to temptation but persevere?

_____

_____

_____

It takes PATIENCE to:

- ☐ Continue to live right before the Lord.
- ☐ Believe Him despite of your circumstances.
- ☐ Trust that He's not going to forsake you.
- ☐ Know that Yahshua is coming again.

There is a reward for our patient continuance in doing what is right in His sight.

But glory, honour, and peace, to every man that worketh good, to the Jew first, and also to the Gentile: 11 For there is no respect of persons with God. Romans 2:10

There are those who delay making a commitment to Christ because they don't want to give up their carnal ways. Then there are those who claim to believe on Him but there is no evidence of change. Do not be deceived, there is a consequence for obeying the law of sin and death.

Examine your ways. Are you more comfortable being a gossiper, stirring up trouble among others, disobeying Yahweh's Word, and being led by unrighteousness, indignation and wrath?

_____

_____

But unto them that are contentious, and do not obey the truth, but obey unrighteousness, indignation and wrath, 9 Tribulation and anguish, upon every soul of man that doeth evil, of the Jew first, and also of the Gentile; Romans 2:8-9

Heavenly Father, please give me a steadfast spirit, to continually pursue Your holiness, that You would get all the glory and honor through my patient surrender. Thank You for the eternal life promised through Your son, Yahshua, in His name, I pray.

Day Seventeen

Prove yourself through your sufferings.

Heavenly Father, You are holy, I glorify You in the beauty of Your Holiness. Thank you for loving, protecting, caring and providing for my family and me. When times are good, I will praise you! When times are difficult, I will praise you! I will honor and exalt You in every circumstance.

Let your kingdom come and will be done in my life, as it is in Heaven. Cause your purpose to be fulfilled in me. I choose to seek you first and invite Precious Holy Spirit to develop His fruit in my life.

Continue to provide for my family, friends, neighbors, and myself all that we need today. May there be more than enough to share with others.

Search my heart, and show me what hidden sin is in my life. As I confess each one to you, purify me in Your presence and create in me a clean heart and renew a right spirit within me.

I forgive my enemies and friends who have hurt, angered, offended or betrayed me and ask that you would have mercy on them and bless them.

Please forgive me of all my evil thoughts, words and actions. I recognize that my sin hurts, angers, offends and betrays You.

Teach me your ways, that I might not sin against You. Inscribe Your word on my heart and mind, that all of my ways, would be pleasing to you.

Do not lead me into temptation, but deliver me from all evil.

To you, Oh Mighty Yahweh, belongs the kingdom, the power and the glory, in Yahshua's name.

For the next seven days, we will dissect and digest 2 Corinthians 6:4-10. The Apostle Paul speaks of how he and the ministers serving alongside him approved themselves, through suffering, to those they were called to serve.

Regardless of what career you have chosen to serve Yahweh in, whatever your title may be, we are each called to reach the lost. Authenticity and Transparency cause people to trust your testimony. People notice your response to the positive and negative occurrences in your life. Your reaction will cause others to see Christ in you or far from you.

But in all things approving ourselves as the ministers of God, in much patience, in afflictions, in necessities, in distresses, 2 Corinthians 6:4

The first way Paul says he proved himself, was through PATIENCE. We are called to be patient with others. You will know that you are growing in this area of your life, when annoyances come and you respond from a place of peace and not anger.

Now we exhort you, brethren, warn them that are unruly, comfort the feebleminded, support the weak, be patient toward all men.
1 Thessalonians 5:14

Are you patient with all people you come in contact with?

_____

Who in your life, is the most difficult to be patient with?

_____

Heavenly Father, please forgive me for my impatience with others. Forgive me for the times I have lashed out in anger and frustration, at those you have placed in my life. I choose to let Your patience shine through me to others, in Yahshua's holy name.

The next way he proves himself is through AFFLICTIONS. These are the painful times in your life. Combine this with NECESSITIES, and things begin to look and feel worst. It is one thing to be struggling and suffering but when you add lack in the picture, things look hopeless. You begin to worry about how bills will be paid, how your children will be fed, if you'll be able to keep your home, and the list can go on for years. Let's not forget to throw in a few DISTRESSES, these are the extreme times of anxiety and pain in your life.

Have you been proving yourself as a servant of Yahweh when you have gone through any of the above? Would you like to prove yourself this way?

_____

_____

Like you, I don't desire any of the above. But, our desire does not change the reality that we all go through hardships. So, we must prove ourselves through our excellent attitude during these times. Next he describes,

In stripes, in imprisonments, in tumults, in labours, in watchings, in fastings; 2 Corinthians 6:5

Have you endured getting unjustly beaten, thrown in jail for the Gospel of Yahshua, commotions, grief, pain, sleepless nights, and hunger?

_____

_____

None of us want to endure struggle, pain, loss, or sacrifice. Yet, those times may come, and our response is important.

Tomorrow, we will learn what helped Paul to prove himself through his many afflictions.

Day Eighteen

Prove yourself through your sufferings continued.

Heavenly Father, You are holy, I glorify You in the beauty of Your Holiness. Thank you for loving, protecting, caring and providing for my family and me. When times are good, I will praise you! When times are difficult, I will praise you! I will honor and exalt You in every circumstance.

Let your kingdom come and will be done in my life, as it is in Heaven. Cause your purpose to be fulfilled in me. I choose to seek you first and invite Precious Holy Spirit to develop His fruit in my life.

Continue to provide for my family, friends, neighbors, and myself all that we need today. May there be more than enough to share with others.

Search my heart, and show me what hidden sin is in my life. As I confess each one to you, purify me in Your presence and create in me a clean heart and renew a right spirit within me.

I forgive my enemies and friends who have hurt, angered, offended or betrayed me and ask that you would have mercy on them and bless them.

Please forgive me of all my evil thoughts, words and actions. I recognize that my sin hurts, angers, offends and betrays You.

Teach me your ways, that I might not sin against You. Inscribe Your word on my heart and mind, that all of my ways, would be pleasing to you.

Do not lead me into temptation, but deliver me from all evil.

To you, Oh Mighty Yahweh, belongs the kingdom, the power and the glory, in Yahshua's name.

By pureness, by knowledge, by long suffering, by
kindness, by the Holy Ghost, by love unfeigned,
2 Corinthians 6:6

To be provoked, yet not respond in inward nor outward anger can only be accomplished through the power of precious Holy Spirit. Paul remained pure, patient, kind and righteous.

PURENESS
And you, that were sometime alienated and enemies
in your mind by wicked works, yet now hath he
reconciled ²² In the body of his flesh through death,
to present you holy and unblameable and
unreproveable in his sight: Colossians 1:21-22

Purity is a choice; a decision to live a life free from sin. It is the conviction that when sin arises in your life it must be removed, not coddled, protected and nurtured.

In Matthew 5:8 Yahshua said,
"Blessed are the pure in heart:
for they shall see God."

Do you want to see Yahweh? I do! We must surrender to the cleansing that comes through His Word and Spirit.

Purity helped Paul endure suffering. Are you living a life of purity?

KNOWLEDGE
The fear of the LORD is the beginning of knowledge,
but fools despise wisdom and instruction.
Proverbs 1:7

Having the knowledge of Yahweh and His will is a vital tool in our gardening kit. Until we get to the place that we truly respect Yahweh, we will lack the wisdom and spiritual understanding we need to excel in every area and season of our lives.

61

For this cause we also, since the day we heard it, do not cease to pray for you, and to desire that ye might be <u>filled with the knowledge of his will in all wisdom and spiritual understanding;</u> 10 That ye might walk worthy of the Lord unto all pleasing, being fruitful in every good work, and <u>increasing in the knowledge of God;</u> 11 Strengthened with all might, according to his glorious power, unto all patience and longsuffering with joyfulness; Colossians 1:9-11

As our knowledge of Yahweh increases, so shall our strength. We will be patient and longsuffering with a JOYFUL attitude!

LONGSUFFERING and KINDNESS
Be kindly affectioned one to another with brotherly love; in honour preferring one another; 11 Not slothful in business; fervent in spirit; serving the Lord; 12 Rejoicing in hope; patient in tribulation; continuing instant in prayer; 13 Distributing to the necessity of saints; given to hospitality. 14 Bless them which persecute you: bless, and curse not. 15 Rejoice with them that do rejoice, and weep with them that weep. Romans 12:10-15

We are not only called to be kind, take care of and bless those who are like minded but we are called to treat our enemies the same way. Even if our enemy is the one who is persecuting us.

Is it difficult to be kind, when going through hardships?

_____

Is it difficult to be kind to your enemies?

_____

Are you ready to adjust your mindset?

_____

Day Nineteen

Prove yourself through your sufferings continued.

Heavenly Father, You are holy, I glorify You in the beauty of Your Holiness. Thank you for loving, protecting, caring and providing for my family and me. When times are good, I will praise you! When times are difficult, I will praise you! I will honor and exalt You in every circumstance.

Let your kingdom come and will be done in my life, as it is in Heaven. Cause your purpose to be fulfilled in me. I choose to seek you first and invite Precious Holy Spirit to develop His fruit in my life.

Continue to provide for my family, friends, neighbors, and myself all that we need today. May there be more than enough to share with others.

Search my heart, and show me what hidden sin is in my life. As I confess each one to you, purify me in Your presence and create in me a clean heart and renew a right spirit within me.

I forgive my enemies and friends who have hurt, angered, offended or betrayed me and ask that you would have mercy on them and bless them.

Please forgive me of all my evil thoughts, words and actions. I recognize that my sin hurts, angers, offends and betrays You.

Teach me your ways, that I might not sin against You. Inscribe Your word on my heart and mind, that all of my ways, would be pleasing to you.

Do not lead me into temptation, but deliver me from all evil.

To you, Oh Mighty Yahweh, belongs the kingdom, the power and the glory, in Yahshua's name.

...by the Holy Ghost, by love unfeigned,
2 Corinthians 6:6

HOLY SPIRIT

When Yahshua was preparing the disciples for His ascension, He explained the necessity of Him leaving so that Holy Spirit, our Comforter, could come. By this, we understand that every believer in Christ needs Holy Spirit to follow in the footsteps of Christ.

Nevertheless I tell you the truth; it is expedient for you that I go away: for if I go not away, the Comforter will not come unto you; but if I depart, I will send him unto you. John 16:7

Meditate on the vital role Holy Spirit played in Yahshua's earthly life, He:
  ➤ Was conceived by Holy Spirit.
  ➤ Was marked by Holy Spirit. *Holy Spirit rested upon Him in the shape of a dove so that John the Baptist could identify Him as Messiah.*
  ➤ Was filled with Holy Spirit.
  ➤ Was led by Holy Spirit.
  ➤ Baptized in the Holy Spirit.
  ➤ Did everything through the Holy Spirit.

But the Comforter, which is the Holy Ghost, whom the Father will send in my name, he shall teach you all things, and bring all things to your remembrance, whatsoever I have said unto you.
John 14:26

Holy Spirit is our comforter, teacher and the one who reminds us of all Yahshua has promised us. Our faith is increased as we pray in Him.

But ye, beloved, building up yourselves on your most holy faith, praying in the Holy Ghost, Jude 20

In Mark 13, Yahshua warned of the sufferings many would endure to spread the gospel among the nations, and promised that Holy Spirit would speak through us, when we do not know what to say.

But take heed to yourselves: for they shall deliver you up to councils; and in the synagogues ye shall be beaten: and ye shall be brought before rulers and kings for my sake, for a testimony against them. 10 And the gospel must first be published among all nations. 11 But when they shall lead you, and deliver you up, take no thought beforehand what ye shall speak, neither do ye premeditate: but whatsoever shall be given you in that hour, that speak ye: <u>for it is not ye that speak, but the Holy Ghost.</u> Mark 13:9-11

If you have not been baptized in the Holy Spirit, just whisper a prayer to the Lord asking Him to baptize and fill you with Holy Spirit in Yahshua's name. It is through Him that we overcome every obstacle in our life and are enabled to comfort others in their hardships. Ask Yahshua to breathe on you as He breathed on the disciples, in John 20:22,

"And when he had said this, he breathed on them, and saith unto them, Receive ye the Holy Ghost:"

LOVE UNFEIGNED

Scripture teaches us that Yahweh is love. As we show genuine love towards others, we prove ourselves as servants of Yahweh.

I challenge you to love God, love others, love yourself and love your enemies. Shine with Genuine Love!

By this shall all men know that ye are my disciples, if ye have love one to another. John 13:35

Reflect on all you have consumed today, what is the Lord saying to you?

Day Twenty

Prove yourself through your sufferings continued.

Heavenly Father, You are holy, I glorify You in the
beauty of Your Holiness. Thank you for loving,
protecting, caring and providing for my family and me.
When times are good, I will praise you! When times are
difficult, I will praise you! I will honor and exalt You in
every circumstance.

Let your kingdom come and will be done in my life, as it
is in Heaven. Cause your purpose to be fulfilled in me. I
choose to seek you first and invite Precious Holy Spirit
to develop His fruit in my life.

Continue to provide for my family, friends, neighbors,
and myself all that we need today. May there be more
than enough to share with others.

Search my heart, and show me what hidden sin is in my
life. As I confess each one to you, purify me in Your
presence and create in me a clean heart and renew a
right spirit within me.

I forgive my enemies and friends who have hurt,
angered, offended or betrayed me and ask that you
would have mercy on them and bless them.

Please forgive me of all my evil thoughts, words and
actions. I recognize that my sin hurts, angers, offends
and betrays You.

Teach me your ways, that I might not sin against You.
Inscribe Your word on my heart and mind, that all of my
ways, would be pleasing to you.

Do not lead me into temptation, but deliver me from all
evil.

To you, Oh Mighty Yahweh, belongs the kingdom, the
power and the glory, in Yahshua's name.

***By the word of truth, by the power of God, by the
armour of righteousness on the right hand and on
the left, 2 Corinthians 6:7***

As we continue to study how Paul and his fellow ministers
were able to prove themselves as Yahweh's servants, we
learn that we are called to live honest lives and speak
truthful words. Remember, we can suffer as a
consequence of righteousness or sin. We must daily
examine our hearts and strive through Holy Spirit to
mature into obedient children of our Heavenly Father. I
warn my children often about lying, teaching them that
their father is not the devil, therefore they should not
behave as he does.

***Ye are of your father the devil, and the lusts of your
father ye will do. He was a murderer from the
beginning, and abode not in the truth, because
there is no truth in him. When he speaketh a lie, he
speaketh of his own: for he is a liar, and the father
of it. John 8:44***

After reading John 8:44, who does your life resemble the
most, Yahweh or satan?

_____

Do you find yourself telling a lot of little "white lies"? If so,
what changes will you make to reflect Yahshua?

_____

_____

WORD OF TRUTH

***But have renounced the hidden things of
dishonesty, not walking in craftiness, nor handling
the word of God deceitfully; but by manifestation of
the truth commending ourselves to every man's
conscience in the sight of God. 2 Corinthians 4:2***

We must renounce deception in every area of our lives. To renounce is to declare to Yahweh and the spiritual forces of darkness that you will no longer engage in such behaviors, thereby making the enemy powerless in your life.

Jesus saith unto him, I am the way, the truth, and the life: no man cometh unto the Father, but by me.
John 14:6

POWER OF GOD

The power of Yahweh is displayed in our lives through righteous living. It is He, who keeps us from sin; causing us to stay the course He has set before us.

Who are kept by the power of God through faith unto salvation ready to be revealed in the last time.
1 Peter 1:5

Yahweh's power preserves us in our times of suffering.

Let the sighing of the prisoner come before thee; according to the greatness of thy power preserve thou those that are appointed to die; Psalm 79:11

We live by the power of Yahweh just as Christ lived through His power.

For though he was crucified through weakness, yet he liveth by the power of God. For we also are weak in him, but we shall live with him by the power of God toward you. 2 Corinthians 13:4

In what ways do you need the POWER OF GOD to manifest in your life?

_____

_____

_____

Day Twenty- One

Prove yourself through your sufferings continued.

Heavenly Father, You are holy, I glorify You in the
beauty of Your Holiness. Thank you for loving,
protecting, caring and providing for my family and me.
When times are good, I will praise you! When times are
difficult, I will praise you! I will honor and exalt You in
every circumstance.

Let your kingdom come and will be done in my life, as it
is in Heaven. Cause your purpose to be fulfilled in me. I
choose to seek you first and invite Precious Holy Spirit
to develop His fruit in my life.

Continue to provide for my family, friends, neighbors,
and myself all that we need today. May there be more
than enough to share with others.

Search my heart, and show me what hidden sin is in my
life. As I confess each one to you, purify me in Your
presence and create in me a clean heart and renew a
right spirit within me.

I forgive my enemies and friends who have hurt,
angered, offended or betrayed me and ask that you
would have mercy on them and bless them.

Please forgive me of all my evil thoughts, words and
actions. I recognize that my sin hurts, angers, offends
and betrays You.

Teach me your ways, that I might not sin against You.
Inscribe Your word on my heart and mind, that all of my
ways, would be pleasing to you.

Do not lead me into temptation, but deliver me from all
evil.

To you, Oh Mighty Yahweh, belongs the kingdom, the
power and the glory, in Yahshua's name.

...by the armour of righteousness on the right hand and on the left, 2 Corinthians 6:7

ARMOUR OF RIGHTEOUSNESS ON BOTH HANDS

We cannot go through our lives oblivious to the fact that we are in a spiritual war. In any war, armor (protective gear) is required. Paul tells us that they had the armor of righteousness in their right and left hands. In Ephesians 6:10-17, he expounds.

Finally, my brethren, be strong in the Lord, and in the power of his might. 11 Put on the whole armour of God, that ye may be able to stand against the wiles of the devil.

We cannot stand against the wiles of the enemy without the armour. Wiles are the strategies he uses to *manipulate or persuade us to do the things that he wants us to do against the will of our Father.* We are commissioned to live righteously through Christ.

12 For we wrestle not against flesh and blood, but against principalities, against powers, against the rulers of the darkness of this world, against spiritual wickedness in high places.

Are people your real enemy, or is there a spiritual realm that you are unable to see, fighting against your purpose and destiny?

_____

_____

13 Wherefore take unto you the whole armour of God, that ye may be able to withstand in the evil day, and having done all, to stand.

Are you fully clothed in the armour, so you can stand?

_____

14 Stand therefore, having your loins girt about with truth, and having on the breastplate of righteousness; 15 And your feet shod with the preparation of the gospel of peace;

Are you walking in truth (honesty), righteousness (right living) and as a carrier of the Gospel of peace?

_____

If you find yourself living, sounding and acting like the devil, then you have fallen to the wiles of the devil. You've been duped, tricked, manipulated and you have given control to the evil one.

16 Above all, taking the shield of faith, wherewith ye shall be able to quench all the fiery darts of the wicked. 17 And take the helmet of salvation, and the sword of the Spirit, which is the word of God:

We need MORE FAITH in YAHSHUA! It is this faith that puts out the scorching arrows of our spiritual enemies. Daily, ask the Lord to increase your faith and to renew your mind to Yahshua's mind. We cannot fight without the S**WORD** of Yahweh's Spirit. Ask Him to give you more wisdom and understanding as you study His Word.

Find every excuse to keep the armour of Yahweh on. It is not designed to be taken off as a physical garment. It is to be worn everywhere you go and even as you sleep. *The armour is a lifestyle of truth, righteousness, peace, faith, salvation and the Word of God.*

What changes will you make to ensure the armour becomes your lifestyle?

_____

_____

_____

Day Twenty- Two

Prove Yourself Through Suffering Continued.

Heavenly Father, You are holy, I glorify You in the beauty of Your Holiness. Thank you for loving, protecting, caring and providing for my family and me. When times are good, I will praise you! When times are difficult, I will praise you! I will honor and exalt You in every circumstance.

Let your kingdom come and will be done in my life, as it is in Heaven. Cause your purpose to be fulfilled in me. I choose to seek you first and invite Precious Holy Spirit to develop His fruit in my life.

Continue to provide for my family, friends, neighbors, and myself all that we need today. May there be more than enough to share with others.

Search my heart, and show me what hidden sin is in my life. As I confess each one to you, purify me in Your presence and create in me a clean heart and renew a right spirit within me.

I forgive my enemies and friends who have hurt, angered, offended or betrayed me and ask that you would have mercy on them and bless them.

Please forgive me of all my evil thoughts, words and actions. I recognize that my sin hurts, angers, offends and betrays You.

Teach me your ways, that I might not sin against You. Inscribe Your word on my heart and mind, that all of my ways, would be pleasing to you.

Do not lead me into temptation, but deliver me from all evil.

To you, Oh Mighty Yahweh, belongs the kingdom, the power and the glory, in Yahshua's name.

By honour and dishonour, by evil report and good report: as deceivers, and yet true; 2 Corinthians 6:8

It is easier to live a life of surrender when you are being honoured, receiving good reports of your health, marriage, children, and career and when others consider you as trustworthy. Those are the periods when you know *you're blessed and highly favored of the Lord.*

Apostle Peter helps us to prepare ourselves for the moments in life when our character will be put on trial, by believers and unbelievers. If you have not been wrongly accused of doing, saying or thinking something that you genuinely were not guilty of, just wait, unfortunately that day will come.

But sanctify the Lord God in your hearts: and be ready always to give an answer to every man that asketh you a reason of the hope that is in you with meekness and fear: Having a good conscience; that, whereas they speak evil of you, as of evildoers, they may be ashamed that falsely accuse your good conversation in Christ. 1 Peter 3:15-16

We are taught, first, to sanctify Yahweh in our hearts.

Daily you are to separate yourself for Him, and allow Him to purify you and make you holy as He is holy.

How are you sanctifying the Lord in your heart, daily?

_____

Next, be ready to humbly and fearfully explain to others, when they ask, why you believe in and serve Yahshua.

Why have you placed your hope in Yahshua?

_____

_____

Lastly, maintain a clean conscience. This entails living right before Yahweh and people, publicly and privately. We are not called to be hypocrites, instead, we are invited to allow Holy Spirit to sanctify us daily. Each day presents new opportunities for growth.

Decide that today:
- ☐ You will surrender more to Yahweh, than you did yesterday.
- ☐ You will be victorious over temptations, unholy compromises and continual sin.

Is your conscience clear?

_____

_____

As Christ's work in your life is evident to others, He will cause those who wrongly accuse you, to be ashamed of speaking evil against you.

Warning! Be careful how you respond to those who speak evil of you. If you spew venomous words, what testimony do you have? If you allow yourself to become contaminated by offense and unforgiveness, it is to your own shame. Guard your heart from evil.

How have you responded to those who have falsely accused you? What is your reaction when you are misrepresented and misjudged?

_____

_____

Let your response always be in LOVE and when you don't know what to say, say nothing at all. At the right time, Holy Spirit will fill your mouth and you will speak.

Quickly forgive, quickly let go, quickly put everything in our Master's hands.

Day Twenty- Three

Prove Yourself Through Suffering Continued.

Heavenly Father, You are holy, I glorify You in the beauty of Your Holiness. Thank you for loving, protecting, caring and providing for my family and me. When times are good, I will praise you! When times are difficult, I will praise you! I will honor and exalt You in every circumstance.

Let your kingdom come and will be done in my life, as it is in Heaven. Cause your purpose to be fulfilled in me. I choose to seek you first and invite Precious Holy Spirit to develop His fruit in my life.

Continue to provide for my family, friends, neighbors, and myself all that we need today. May there be more than enough to share with others.

Search my heart, and show me what hidden sin is in my life. As I confess each one to you, purify me in Your presence and create in me a clean heart and renew a right spirit within me.

I forgive my enemies and friends who have hurt, angered, offended or betrayed me and ask that you would have mercy on them and bless them.

Please forgive me of all my evil thoughts, words and actions. I recognize that my sin hurts, angers, offends and betrays You.

Teach me your ways, that I might not sin against You. Inscribe Your word on my heart and mind, that all of my ways, would be pleasing to you.

Do not lead me into temptation, but deliver me from all evil.

To you, Oh Mighty Yahweh, belongs the kingdom, the power and the glory, in Yahshua's name.

As unknown, and yet well known; as dying, and, behold, we live; ... 2 Corinthians 6:9

UNKNOWN YET WELL KNOWN

The word *unknown*, used in the above passage, in the Greek is *agnoeō*, meaning to be ignorant, to not understand. The phrase, *yet well known*, in the Greek is *epiginōskō*, which is to be fully acquainted with, to know thoroughly or accurately. What is Paul saying, when he speaks of being unknown yet well known?

Paul and his fellow ministers would be sent by Yahweh to territories that had not been reached with the Gospel of Christ. They were certainly unknown, misunderstood and appeared strange to the communities they were sent to. They also experienced this in territories where they were known and their good works were evil spoken of.

Yet, among themselves and the body of believers, they knew the purity of one another's motives in serving Yahshua. Although this encouraged their hearts, the most encouragement came in knowing that they were WELL KNOWN by Yahshua.

> *If the world hate you, ye know that it hated me before it hated you. 19 If ye were of the world, the world would love his own: but because ye are not of the world, but I have chosen you out of the world, therefore the world hateth you. 20 Remember the word that I said unto you, the servant is not greater than his lord. If they have persecuted me, they will also persecute you; if they have kept my saying, they will keep yours also. 21 But all these things will they do unto you for my name's sake, because they know not him that sent me. John 15:18-21*

Yahshua explains that we will be persecuted because people do not KNOW YAHWEH. We should desire to be KNOWN by Yahshua, our Lord and Savior, more than being known by others. He warns us in Matthew 7:21-23,

76

"Not every one that saith unto me, Lord, Lord, shall enter into the kingdom of heaven; but he that doeth the will of my Father which is in heaven. 22 Many will say to me in that day, Lord, Lord, have we not prophesied in thy name? And in thy name have cast out devils? And in thy name done many wonderful works? 23 And then will I profess unto them, I never knew you: depart from me, ye that work iniquity."

Are you known by Yahshua?

_____

_____

_____

DYING YET LIVING

Our relationship with Christ is a growing experience. To grow and bear fruit, like any seed, we must die. Our flesh must die daily as our Spirit matures and is strengthened in His presence.

For we would not, brethren, have you ignorant of our trouble which came to us in Asia, that we were pressed out of measure, above strength, insomuch that we despaired even of life: 9 But we had the sentence of death in ourselves, that we should not trust in ourselves, but in God which raiseth the dead: 10 Who delivered us from so great a death, and doth deliver: in whom we trust that he will yet deliver us; 2 Corinthians 1:8-10

Are you willing to stop trusting in yourself and trust in Yahweh completely, the one who resurrects the dead, delivers us from evil and promises eternal life?

_____

_____

77

Day Twenty- Four

Prove yourself through your sufferings continued.

Heavenly Father, You are holy, I glorify You in the beauty of Your Holiness. Thank you for loving, protecting, caring and providing for my family and me. When times are good, I will praise you! When times are difficult, I will praise you! I will honor and exalt You in every circumstance.

Let your kingdom come and will be done in my life, as it is in Heaven. Cause your purpose to be fulfilled in me. I choose to seek you first and invite Precious Holy Spirit to develop His fruit in my life.

Continue to provide for my family, friends, neighbors, and myself all that we need today. May there be more than enough to share with others.

Search my heart, and show me what hidden sin is in my life. As I confess each one to you, purify me in Your presence and create in me a clean heart and renew a right spirit within me.

I forgive my enemies and friends who have hurt, angered, offended or betrayed me and ask that you would have mercy on them and bless them.

Please forgive me of all my evil thoughts, words and actions. I recognize that my sin hurts, angers, offends and betrays You.

Teach me your ways, that I might not sin against You. Inscribe Your word on my heart and mind, that all of my ways, would be pleasing to you.

Do not lead me into temptation, but deliver me from all evil.

To you, Oh Mighty Yahweh, belongs the kingdom, the power and the glory, in Yahshua's name.

"...as chastened, and not killed; [10] *As sorrowful, yet alway rejoicing; 2 Corinthians 6:9-10*

AS CHASTENED YET NOT KILLED

In Paul's testimony, he and his fellow ministers were beaten close to death for their commitment to Yahshua. Per OpenDoorsUSA.org as of 2017, each month, *322 Christians are killed for their faith, 214 churches and Christian properties are destroyed and 722 forms of violence are committed against Christians.* Do these statistics surprise you? Are you one who has been beaten for your faith in Christ?

For unto you it is given in the behalf of Christ, not only to believe on him, but also to suffer for his sake; [30] *having the same conflict which ye saw in me, and now hear to be in me. Philippians 1:29-30*

The Philippians were experiencing the same suffering they saw and heard in Paul. Paul understood that Yahshua shows His longsuffering through His people. Since, Christ used Paul as a pattern of suffering for those of us who would later come to believe on Yahshua, we should all expect to suffer at some point in our journey.

Do any of your trials make you feel worn down to the point of death?

_____

_____

_____

This is a faithful saying, and worthy of all acceptation, that Christ Jesus came into the world to save sinners; of whom I am chief. [16] *Howbeit for this cause I obtained mercy, that in me first Jesus Christ might shew forth all longsuffering, for a pattern to them which should hereafter believe on him to life everlasting.* [17] *Now unto the King eternal, immortal, invisible, the only wise God, be honour and glory for ever and ever. 1 Timothy 1:15-17*

Are you willing to suffer so that Christ can be seen through you?

_____

_____

_____

SORROWFUL YET ALWAYS REJOICING

Who now rejoice in my sufferings for you, and fill up that which is behind of the afflictions of Christ in my flesh for his body's sake, which is the church: Colossians 1:24

Is it possible that a person can genuinely rejoice during their times of suffering? It is very possible. Why? Because when you receive a revelation of the purpose of your suffering, you understand that Christ is glorified and the body of Christ is edified.

Paul had every reason to be depressed and filled with sorrow, yet every time he chose joy. Joy shifts the atmosphere and brings the focus back on Yahshua and not on our sorrows.

Do you know anyone who chooses not to complain but rejoices in their hardships? If yes, reach out to him/her today and ask them why and how they became like that.

_____

_____

Heavenly Father please remove my fear of suffering for your glory and fill me with your joy when I am surrounded by many sorrows, in Yahshua's name.

Day Twenty- Five

Prove yourself through your sufferings continued.

Heavenly Father, You are holy, I glorify You in the beauty of Your Holiness. Thank you for loving, protecting, caring and providing for my family and me. When times are good, I will praise you! When times are difficult, I will praise you! I will honor and exalt You in every circumstance.

Let your kingdom come and will be done in my life, as it is in Heaven. Cause your purpose to be fulfilled in me. I choose to seek you first and invite Precious Holy Spirit to develop His fruit in my life.

Continue to provide for my family, friends, neighbors, and myself all that we need today. May there be more than enough to share with others.

Search my heart, and show me what hidden sin is in my life. As I confess each one to you, purify me in Your presence and create in me a clean heart and renew a right spirit within me.

I forgive my enemies and friends who have hurt, angered, offended or betrayed me and ask that you would have mercy on them and bless them.

Please forgive me of all my evil thoughts, words and actions. I recognize that my sin hurts, angers, offends and betrays You.

Teach me your ways, that I might not sin against You. Inscribe Your word on my heart and mind, that all of my ways, would be pleasing to you.

Do not lead me into temptation, but deliver me from all evil.

To you, Oh Mighty Yahweh, belongs the kingdom, the power and the glory, in Yahshua's name.

...as poor, yet making many rich; as having nothing, and yet possessing all things."
2 Corinthians 6:10

AS POOR YET MAKING MANY RICH

Is there anything wrong with having an abundance of wealth? Absolutely not! To those the Lord entrusts with great financial wealth, He expects them to obey all that He commands them to do with what is entrusted. For example, if He tells you to sell all you have, give it away and follow Him, would you?

_____

Jesus said unto him, If thou wilt be perfect, go and sell that thou hast, and give to the poor, and thou shalt have treasure in heaven: and come and follow me. Matthew 19:21

We must be cautious so as not to make money our god. According to Matthew 6:33, as we seek the Kingdom of Yahweh first and His righteousness, everything we need will be provided. Place more focus on storing up treasure in heaven than on the earth.

He that trusteth in his riches shall fall; but the righteous shall flourish as a branch.
Proverbs 11:28

What does Paul mean when He says, "as poor, yet making many rich"? How can we enrich the lives of others?

_____

_____

_____

There is that maketh himself rich, yet hath nothing: there is that maketh himself poor, yet hath great riches. Proverbs 13:7

In Luke 12:15-21, Yahshua warns us to be careful of covetousness and not to measure our worth by our possessions. He shares a parable of a rich man, who had more than he knew what to do with, so he stored up his possessions and decided he should relax and enjoy life without a worry. Let's pick up at verses 20-21, "**But God said unto him, Thou fool, this night thy soul shall be required of thee: then whose shall those things be, which thou hast provided? 21 So is he that layeth up treasure for himself, and is not rich toward God.**"

Are you rich towards Yahweh? In Christ, we have the joy of sharing the promised abundant life with others, we are made spiritually rich through our faith. As we share the gospel of Yahshua our Messiah with others, they become rich, when they invite Him to be Lord of their lives.

HAVING NOTHING YET HAVING ALL THINGS

But what things were gain to me, those I counted loss for Christ. 8 Yea doubtless, and I count all things but loss for the excellency of the knowledge of Christ Jesus my Lord: for whom I have suffered the loss of all things, and do count them but dung, that I may win Christ, Philippians 3:7-8

What a picture this paints in my mind! Imagine everything you lose or let go of for Christ is equivalent to dung. All our material possessions fail in comparison to the glory of KNOWING YAHSHUA.

Is your mindset shifting as it concerns your wealth and possessions?

_____

_____

_____

Day Twenty-Six

Patience Requires Humility.

Heavenly Father, You are holy, I glorify You in the beauty of Your Holiness. Thank you for loving, protecting, caring and providing for my family and me. When times are good, I will praise you! When times are difficult, I will praise you! I will honor and exalt You in every circumstance.

Let your kingdom come and will be done in my life, as it is in Heaven. Cause your purpose to be fulfilled in me. I choose to seek you first and invite Precious Holy Spirit to develop His fruit in my life.

Continue to provide for my family, friends, neighbors, and myself all that we need today. May there be more than enough to share with others.

Search my heart, and show me what hidden sin is in my life. As I confess each one to you, purify me in Your presence and create in me a clean heart and renew a right spirit within me.

I forgive my enemies and friends who have hurt, angered, offended or betrayed me and ask that you would have mercy on them and bless them.

Please forgive me of all my evil thoughts, words and actions. I recognize that my sin hurts, angers, offends and betrays You.

Teach me your ways, that I might not sin against You. Inscribe Your word on my heart and mind, that all of my ways, would be pleasing to you.

Do not lead me into temptation, but deliver me from all evil.

To you, Oh Mighty Yahweh, belongs the kingdom, the power and the glory, in Yahshua's name.

"We note from Paul that the thorn was given to keep him humble. In Ecclesiastes 7:8, Solomon teaches us that patience is better than pride, "The end of a thing is better than its beginning; the patient in spirit is better than the proud in spirit." The Hebrew word used here is arek, meaning patient, slow to anger. I had never thought to compare a patient spirit to a proud spirit, it implies that a patient person is humble and slow to anger, while an impatient person is a gabah (in Hebrew), one who is high or proud, showing arrogant superiority to and disdain of those one views as unworthy. 1 Peter 5:5-11 instructs us that Yahweh gives grace to the humble and resist the proud, therefore we must clothe ourselves in humility." (Marcellus, Developing the Fruit of the Spirit, A Journey Through the Heart of Christ p.99)

I encourage you to regularly assess your pride and anger levels. Pay attention to your responses to situations and private thoughts of how you view others.

Do you control your anger or does anger control you?

_____

Do you think more highly of yourself than you do others?

_____

As the Fruit of Patience/Longsuffering is being produced in your life, it will eat away at the pride of life. Embrace the process, it will make you a clearer reflection of Yahshua to others.

For all that is in the world, the lust of the flesh, and the lust of the eyes, and the pride of life, is not of the Father, but is of the world. 1 John 2:16

Yahshua humbled Himself of His Divine reputation, taking on the flesh of humanity, to suffer and die for mankind. Therefore, we should be motivated and inspired to take off our pride and put on His humility.

But we see Jesus, who was made a little lower than the angels <u>for the suffering of death</u>, crowned with glory and honour; that he by the grace of God should taste death for every man. Hebrews 2:9

Are you willing to take off your pride and put on patience and humility?

To be like Christ, we must take on His way of thinking and perceiving. At the last Supper, He knelt to wash His disciples' feet; to Peter this idea was absurd. Yet, Yahshua shifted their mindsets to understand that to lead well, one must serve, laying down their life for others.

<u>Let this mind be in you</u>, which was also in Christ Jesus: 6 Who, being in the form of God, thought it not robbery to be equal with God: 7 But made himself of no reputation, and took upon him the form of a servant, and was made in the likeness of men: 8 And being found in fashion as a man, <u>he humbled himself</u>, and <u>became obedient unto death, even the death of the cross</u>. Philippians 2:5-8

Humility produces obedience. To endure suffering one must surrender completely to the will of Yahweh, trusting that His way and plan is higher than your own.

Heavenly Father, forgive me for the lust of the flesh, lust of the eyes and the pride of life. Make me patient in spirit and remove haughtiness from my heart. Let me think as You think, cause me to see through Your eyes. Shift every mindset that blocks me from embracing Your longsuffering, in Yahshua's name.

I therefore, the prisoner of the Lord, beseech you that ye walk worthy of the vocation wherewith ye are called, 2 with all lowliness and meekness, with longsuffering, forbearing one another in love; Ephesians 4:1-2

Day Twenty-Seven

Patience and Comfort of the Word Bring Hope.

Heavenly Father, You are holy, I glorify You in the beauty of Your Holiness. Thank you for loving, protecting, caring and providing for my family and me. When times are good, I will praise you! When times are difficult, I will praise you! I will honor and exalt You in every circumstance.

Let your kingdom come and will be done in my life, as it is in Heaven. Cause your purpose to be fulfilled in me. I choose to seek you first and invite Precious Holy Spirit to develop His fruit in my life.

Continue to provide for my family, friends, neighbors, and myself all that we need today. May there be more than enough to share with others.

Search my heart, and show me what hidden sin is in my life. As I confess each one to you, purify me in Your presence and create in me a clean heart and renew a right spirit within me.

I forgive my enemies and friends who have hurt, angered, offended or betrayed me and ask that you would have mercy on them and bless them.

Please forgive me of all my evil thoughts, words and actions. I recognize that my sin hurts, angers, offends and betrays You.

Teach me your ways, that I might not sin against You. Inscribe Your word on my heart and mind, that all of my ways, would be pleasing to you.

Do not lead me into temptation, but deliver me from all evil.

To you, Oh Mighty Yahweh, belongs the kingdom, the power and the glory, in Yahshua's name.

Blessed be God, even the Father of our Lord Jesus Christ, the Father of mercies, and the God of all comfort; 4 Who comforteth us in all our tribulation, that we may be able to comfort them which are in any trouble, by the comfort wherewith we ourselves are comforted of God. 2 Corinthians 1:3-4

This scripture brings the most solace to me, when I don't have the answers as to why things are happening in my life that are painful, uncomfortable and displeasurable. I am reminded that in my pain, I have the pleasure of experiencing the support of our Heavenly Father. He holds my hand and walks me through, speaking words of comfort, mercy and peace. It is through these unforgettable encounters with Him, that we learn how to comfort others. Thank Yahweh for tribulations, because through them we experience another facet of our Maker and Lover of our Souls.

For as the sufferings of Christ abound in us, so our consolation also aboundeth by Christ. 6 And whether we be afflicted, it is for your consolation and salvation, which is effectual in the enduring of the same sufferings which we also suffer: or whether we be comforted, it is for your consolation and salvation. 7 And our hope of you is stedfast, knowing, that as ye are partakers of the sufferings, so shall ye be also of the consolation.
2 Corinthians 1:5-7

The greater our suffering, the greater our consolation. As Paul wrote above, the suffering he endured produced the comfort and salvation for others. His hope was steadfast knowing that any who partook in the sufferings would also partake of the consolation.

I am thankful for every word recorded throughout scripture. They teach, comfort and produce HOPE in us.

For whatsoever things were written aforetime were written for our learning, that we through patience

***and comfort of the scriptures might have hope.
Romans 15:4***

Our Heavenly Father understands the issues of our hearts and allows us to experience Him as a God of Patience and Comfort. He desires that we be like minded.

What scripture(s) brings you the most comfort?

_____

Now the God of patience and consolation grant you to be likeminded one toward another according to Christ Jesus: ⁶ that ye may with one mind and one mouth glorify God, even the Father of our Lord Jesus Christ. Romans 15:5-6

When you understand that your times of waiting and suffering are assigned by Yahweh, you will no longer walk through life in a state of unruly panic mixed with feeling sorry for yourself. Remember, trials and tribulations test our faith. These tests produce patience and when patience is complete, WE LACK NOTHING. Through them, Holy Spirit, exposes and removes wrong thinking, perfects His character in us and prepares us for a new chapter in Him.

The result of patience looks like, a complete you. In Matthew 5, Yahshua gives us an outline of the Blessings from our Heavenly Father. In verse 48 He closes with,

"Be ye therefore perfect, even as your Father which is in heaven is perfect."

The Goal of Patience is to make us into a PERFECT reflection of our Heavenly Father. How awesome is that?

Heavenly Father, let my life reflect Your glory. Help me to keep my eyes on Yahshua, during the times You've assigned for my faith to be tried by the heat of suffering. Make me complete in You, in Yahshua's name.

89

Day Twenty-Eight

Yahweh will deliver you from the Pit.

Heavenly Father, You are holy, I glorify You in the beauty of Your Holiness. Thank you for loving, protecting, caring and providing for my family and me. When times are good, I will praise you! When times are difficult, I will praise you! I will honor and exalt You in every circumstance.

Let your kingdom come and will be done in my life, as it is in Heaven. Cause your purpose to be fulfilled in me. I choose to seek you first and invite Precious Holy Spirit to develop His fruit in my life.

Continue to provide for my family, friends, neighbors, and myself all that we need today. May there be more than enough to share with others.

Search my heart, and show me what hidden sin is in my life. As I confess each one to you, purify me in Your presence and create in me a clean heart and renew a right spirit within me.

I forgive my enemies and friends who have hurt, angered, offended or betrayed me and ask that you would have mercy on them and bless them.

Please forgive me of all my evil thoughts, words and actions. I recognize that my sin hurts, angers, offends and betrays You.

Teach me your ways, that I might not sin against You. Inscribe Your word on my heart and mind, that all of my ways, would be pleasing to you.

Do not lead me into temptation, but deliver me from all evil.

To you, Oh Mighty Yahweh, belongs the kingdom, the power and the glory, in Yahshua's name.

During the darkest times in our lives, we cry and plead for Yahweh to rescue us from the pit. David says that he waited patiently on the Lord, as he was in his own horrible pit.

I waited patiently for the LORD; and he inclined unto me, and heard my cry. Psalm 40:1

There are times when Yahweh does not immediately rescue us. We may have to sit in the miry clay for a little while. Joseph was thrown in a waterless cistern by his brothers, where he sat for a little while, only to be pulled out and sold into slavery for 20 pieces of silver. (Genesis 37)

Have you gone through any dark periods of your life?

_____

Are you in your darkest period now? _____

Is it/was it at the hands of someone who has betrayed you?

_____

_____

David was crying before the Lord and yet he says he was waiting patiently. *Our tears do not represent impatience, just as our persistent prayers do not represent unbelief.* Just as the Lord responded to David, He will respond to you. The fruit of patience longsuffering attracts the Lord's attention.

Let's look at the result of patience in David's life.

"He brought me up also out of an horrible pit, out of the miry clay, and set my feet upon a rock, and established my goings." Psalm 40:2

When the Lord brought him out, he was ESTABLISHED. When the Lord brought Joseph out of the cistern, slavery and prison, he was ESTABLISHED! Yahweh will ESTABLISH you, when He pulls you from your pit.

And he hath put a new song in my mouth, even praise unto our God: many shall see it, and fear, and shall trust in the LORD. Psalm 40:3

The Lord will give you a new song, even a praise song. Your song, is the testimony of what and how Yahweh brought you through. You won't look, speak or be the same. Joseph's brothers didn't recognize him. (Genesis 42) Your testimony will cause people to fear Yahweh and have faith in Him.

Hebrews 12:1-2 encourages us,

"Wherefore seeing we also are compassed about with so great a cloud of witnesses, let us lay aside every weight, and the sin which doth so easily beset us, and let us run with patience the race that is set before us, 2 Looking unto Jesus the author and finisher of our faith; who for the joy that was set before him endured the cross, despising the shame, and is set down at the right hand of the throne of God.

Don't allow your pit, the weights of life you carry or the sin you struggle with to cloud your focus any longer. Lay them aside, give them to Yahshua! Then you will be able to run this race with patience, as your eyes are completely fixed on Him.

Heavenly Father, as I cry to You, I know You hear me. Holy Spirit help me to be patient, focused and faithful, when I walk through the difficult moments in my life. Put a new song in mouth, not one of complaining, but one of victory and praise. Establish me, in every area of my life, for Your Glory. Thank You, in Yahshua's name.

Day Twenty-Nine
Faith and Patience cause you to inherit the promises of Yahweh!

Heavenly Father, You are holy, I glorify You in the beauty of Your Holiness. Thank you for loving, protecting, caring and providing for my family and me. When times are good, I will praise you! When times are difficult, I will praise you! I will honor and exalt You in every circumstance.

Let your kingdom come and will be done in my life, as it is in Heaven. Cause your purpose to be fulfilled in me. I choose to seek you first and invite Precious Holy Spirit to develop His fruit in my life.

Continue to provide for my family, friends, neighbors, and myself all that we need today. May there be more than enough to share with others.

Search my heart, and show me what hidden sin is in my life. As I confess each one to you, purify me in Your presence and create in me a clean heart and renew a right spirit within me.

I forgive my enemies and friends who have hurt, angered, offended or betrayed me and ask that you would have mercy on them and bless them.

Please forgive me of all my evil thoughts, words and actions. I recognize that my sin hurts, angers, offends and betrays You.

Teach me your ways, that I might not sin against You. Inscribe Your word on my heart and mind, that all of my ways, would be pleasing to you.

Do not lead me into temptation, but deliver me from all evil.

To you, Oh Mighty Yahweh, belongs the kingdom, the power and the glory, in Yahshua's name.

To you, Oh Mighty Yahweh, belongs the kingdom, the power and the glory, in Yahshua's name.

And we desire that every one of you do shew the same diligence to the full assurance of hope unto the end: 12 That ye be not slothful, but followers of them who through faith and patience inherit the promises. Hebrews 6:11-12

Often, we begin well in our pursuit and worship of Yahshua, but when difficult times arise and promises seem to be delayed, our passion may begin to dwindle.

We are warned to press on, as those who through their faith and patience received the inheritance of Yahweh's promises. Do not become slothful, sluggish and slow as you wait on the manifestation of Yahweh's promises.

Do your trials and tribulations:

   1. Cause you to trust Yahweh more?

_____

   2. Cause you to question Yahweh's promises?

_____

   3. Cause you to lose your passion and become indifferent towards Yahweh?

_____

Abraham was a man of Yahweh who after patiently enduring, he obtained the promise! Have you considered how long Abraham waited to have his "promised child" from the womb of his wife Sarah?

He was 75 years old when our Lord promised to make him a great nation (Gen. 12). Years passed and we get to Gen 15, when Yahweh clarified that Abraham's heir will come from his own loins. We observe Sarai getting impatient, feeling responsible for the Lord not giving them an heir. She thought He had prevented her from having children, so she gave Abram, Hagar, her Egyptian maidservant, and Ishmael was conceived.

In your anxiety have you tried to help God fulfill His promise?

Abram was 86 years old when Ishmael was born, this was 11 years after the initial promise. When Abram was 99 years old (**24 years after the initial promise**) our God El Shaddai appeared to him (Gen. 17), gave him the terms of the covenant, changed he and his wife's name to Abraham and Sarah and declared that Sarah would have a son (Isaac). Just as the Lord had promised, at 100 years old Abraham fathered Isaac born from Sarah when she was 90 years old.

For when God made promise to Abraham, because he could swear by no greater, he sware by himself, 14 saying, Surely blessing I will bless thee, and multiplying I will multiply thee. 15 And so, after he had patiently endured, he obtained the promise. Hebrews 6:13-15

How many years have you been waiting on a promise from Yahweh?

Have you been patient during your time of waiting?

After 25 years, Abraham received the promise. Be encouraged, don't stop believing, continue to patiently wait, what Yahweh promised will come to pass.

So shall my word be that goeth forth out of my mouth: it shall not return unto me void, but it shall accomplish that which I please, and it shall prosper in the thing whereto I sent it. Isaiah 55:11

Day Thirty

Putting Patience Longsuffering into action.

Heavenly Father, You are holy, I glorify You in the beauty of Your Holiness. Thank you for loving, protecting, caring and providing for my family and me. When times are good, I will praise you! When times are difficult, I will praise you! I will honor and exalt You in every circumstance.

Let your kingdom come and will be done in my life, as it is in Heaven. Cause your purpose to be fulfilled in me. I choose to seek you first and invite Precious Holy Spirit to develop His fruit in my life.

Continue to provide for my family, friends, neighbors, and myself all that we need today. May there be more than enough to share with others.

Search my heart, and show me what hidden sin is in my life. As I confess each one to you, purify me in Your presence and create in me a clean heart and renew a right spirit within me.

I forgive my enemies and friends who have hurt, angered, offended or betrayed me and ask that you would have mercy on them and bless them.

Please forgive me of all my evil thoughts, words and actions. I recognize that my sin hurts, angers, offends and betrays You.

Teach me your ways, that I might not sin against You. Inscribe Your word on my heart and mind, that all of my ways, would be pleasing to you.

Do not lead me into temptation, but deliver me from all evil.

To you, Oh Mighty Yahweh, belongs the kingdom, the power and the glory, in Yahshua's name.

To you, Oh Mighty Yahweh, belongs the kingdom, the power and the glory, in Yahshua's name.

For twenty-nine days, you have examined some of the ways and purposes our Heavenly Father uses the Fruit of Patience Longsuffering our lives. Meditate on all you have learned, as you prepare to evaluate your growth and write your testimony.

Our Lord waits patiently on us, to develop His Fruit.

The Lord's longsuffering is Salvation. If He were not patient with us, we would be eternally condemned.

Creation Waits Patiently on Us to realize, believe and walk in who we are in Yahshua.

When you are not watchful, *Impatience leads you to disobedience and idolatry.*

Why Are You Suffering? Is it because of unrepentant sin or submission to righteous living?

Don't be surprised if you are called to suffer, for the sake of righteousness.

Don't be afraid to suffer for what is right, Yahweh has given you a Spirit of power, love and a sound mind.

Christ left us an example of suffering, therefore model your attitude about suffering after His.

Be aware, *Temptation is a type of suffering,* don't be discouraged by it, neither give in to it.

Arm Yourself with the Mind of Christ. View hardships as gifts from our Heavenly Father to remove your sin nature.

It is easy to take your frustrations out on others. *Do not mistreat others in your times of suffering.*

We can *Suffer with Joy and Patience*, when we are filled with Holy Spirit.

Be sober and vigilant in your times of suffering; don't let the pain intoxicate and blur your vision.

Let Patience Have Its Perfect Work.
Your fiery trials will refine your faith and purify you.

Rest in the Lord, free from fear, anger and jealousy.
Don't be distracted by those who prosper by unrighteous gain, Yahweh is Just.

Continue to do what is righteous as you wait.
Examine yourself and renounce hidden sin in your life.

Prove yourself through your sufferings:

✓ *Much Patience, Afflictions, Necessities, Distresses*
✓ *In stripes, imprisonments, tumults, labours, watching, fasting*
✓ *Pureness, Knowledge, Longsuffering, Kindness, Holy Spirit, Love unfeigned*
✓ *Word of truth, Power of Yahweh, Armour of Righteousness*
✓ *Don't be moved when people dishonour, give evil reports of you and lie about you.*
✓ *Unknown yet known by Yahshua, dying in the Flesh but living in the Spirit, chastened yet not killed*
✓ *Sorrowful, yet always rejoicing, Poor, yet making many rich, having nothing, yet possessing all things*

Patience Requires Humility.
Humility produces obedience.

Patience and Comfort of the Word Bring Hope.
Comfort others with the comfort the Lord comforts you.

Yahweh will deliver you from your pit; *and ESTABLISH every area of your life.*

Faith and Patience cause you to inherit the promises of Yahweh! *Don't be discouraged by the waiting period.*

PERSONAL EVALUATION

How often do you...	Never	Sometimes	Always
Obey Yahweh?			
Reflect on how patient Yahweh is with you?			
Give up on/Lose hope in the promises of Yahweh?			
Walk in Your Identity?			
Struggle with being impatient?			
Struggle with idolatry?			
Suffer for wrong doing?			
Suffer for doing what is right?			
Resist temptation?			
Mistreat others when having a difficult day?			
Have a joyous attitude during a difficult day?			
Feel overwhelmed by difficult times?			
Rest in the Lord as you wait on Him?			
Grow tired of doing what's right?			
Depend on Holy Spirit?			
Wear the Armour of Yahweh?			

Wow! Can you believe the changes Holy Spirit has made in your life? Help cement it by giving glory to Yahweh with your testimony about the results of this journey.

_____

_____

_____

Visit **WWW.SUZANNEMARCELLUS.COM** to avail yourself of other books in the Developing the Fruit of the Spirit, A Journey Through the Heart of Christ series, written by Suzanne Phillippa Marcellus.

Developing the Fruit of the Spirit, A Journey Through the Heart of Christ

(Available in print and audio)

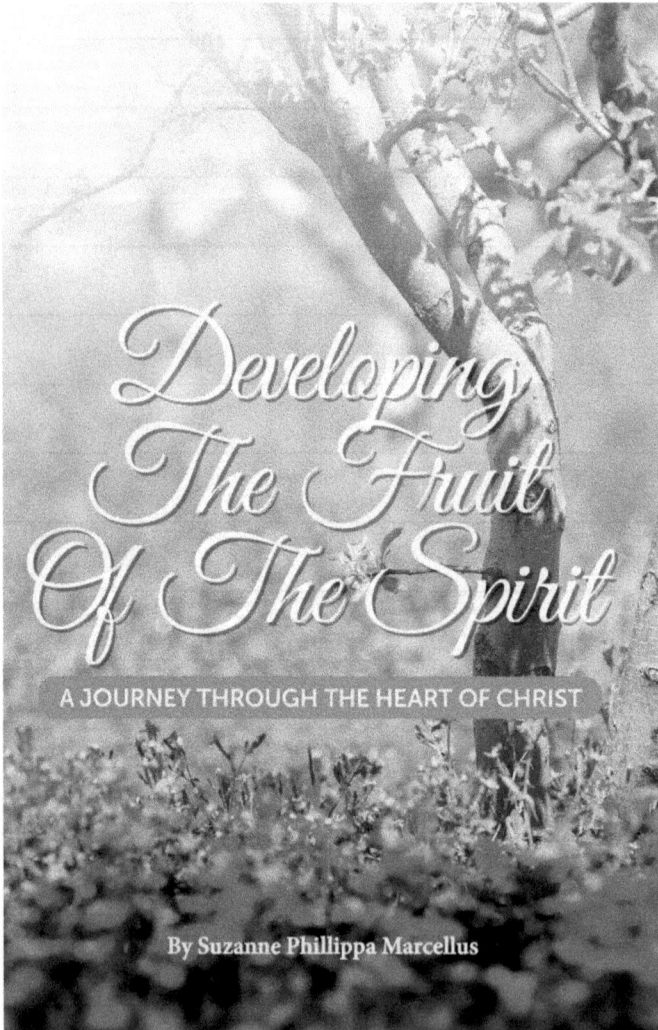

Developing the Fruit of Love
30 Day Devotional

Developing the Fruit of Joy
30 Day Devotional

Developing the Fruit of Peace
30 Day Devotional

Developing the Fruit of Patience Longsuffering
30 Day Devotional

Developing the Fruit of Kindness
30 Day Devotional

Developing the Fruit of Goodness
30 Day Devotional

Developing the Fruit of Faithfulness Faith
30 Day Devotional

Developing the Fruit of Gentleness Meekness
30 Day Devotional

Developing the Fruit of Self-Control
30 Day Devotional

Developing the Fruit of Righteousness
30 Day Devotional

Developing the Fruit of Justice
30 Day Devotional

Developing the Fruit of Mercy
30 Day Devotional

MORE ABOUT THE AUTHOR

Suzanne was given a vision by the Lord in 2002 to counsel, disciple, educate and house hurting children and teens. House of Protection, Inc., a Christian, non-denominational, not-for-profit 501(C) 3 organization, was birth on May 25, 2004.

WWW.HOUSEOFPROTECTION.ORG

We are a refuge of hope for children, teens and their families, providing Pastoral Counseling, Community Workshops and a future Residential Program.

MISSION STATEMENT
To Reach, Rehabilitate, and Restore troubled youth and their families with the love of God and the teachings of Christ Jesus, our Lord.

VISION
The primary purpose of House of Protection, Inc. is to be a Christian residential rehabilitation program for troubled boys and girls ages 5-18 in South Florida. We are committed to providing a safe home, individual and family counseling, and an education based on God's Word. Our goal is to restore the youth to their families based on Luke 1:17, *"And he will go on before the Lord, in the Spirit and power of Elijah, to turn the hearts of the fathers to the children and the disobedient to the wisdom of the righteous-to make ready a people prepared for the Lord"*. Our vision is that through Biblical training and counseling restoration will take place in the youth and in their families. This will result in these children and teens becoming positive role models and contributing members of society.

www.ingramcontent.com/pod-product-compliance
Lightning Source LLC
Chambersburg PA
CBHW071618040426
42452CB00009B/1384